Revamp

A MEMOIR OF TRAVEL AND
OBSESSIVE RENOVATION

PAMELA REYNOLDS

Black Rose Writing | Texas

©2020 by Pamela Reynolds
All rights reserved. No part of this book may be reproduced, stored in a retrieval system or transmitted in any form or by any means without the prior written permission of the publishers, except by a reviewer who may quote brief passages in a review to be printed in a newspaper, magazine or journal.

The author grants the final approval for this literary material.

First printing

This is a work of creative nonfiction. While all the stories in this book are true, some names and identifying details have been changed to protect the privacy of the people involved. Conversations in the book all come from the author's recollections and are not word-for-word transcripts. Rather, the author has retold them in a way that evokes the feeling and meaning of what was said.

ISBN: 978-1-68433-418-6
PUBLISHED BY BLACK ROSE WRITING
www.blackrosewriting.com

Printed in the United States of America
Suggested Retail Price (SRP) $17.95

Revamp is printed in Sabon

*As a planet-friendly publisher, Black Rose Writing does its best to eliminate unnecessary waste to reduce paper usage and energy costs, while never compromising the reading experience. As a result, the final word count vs. page count may not meet common expectations.

*FOR THOSE EVERYWHERE SEEKING BEAUTY,
AT HOME AND IN LIFE.*

Praise for
Revamp

"Beautifully constructed, evocative, and emotional, this author's first non-fiction story will capture your heart and mind. Read it, and you will find yourself there too. It shouts: When is the movie coming out?"
–Karen Gross, author and educator; former President of Southern Vermont College and Senior Advisor to the U.S. Department of Education

"A delightful tale embodying both the American and Italian fascination with house and home."
–Plinio Innocenzi, author of *The Innovators Behind Leonardo*

"It was so absorbing. AND the writing is terrific. I feel like I just finished a huge bag of potato chips and lost track of time."
–Jane Simon, former graphic designer, *The Boston Globe*

"A wisdom-filled memoir that doubles as a sweeping travelogue reaching from Boston to Sardinia and back again. Gorgeously written and culturally astute."
–Matthew Gilbert, TV critic, *The Boston Globe*

Revamp

Original ground level

- The Monster's place
- bath
- living room
- to the cantina
- gate
- carport
- driveway
- veranda
- kitchen dining
- bed room
- bedroom
- oleanders
- well
- lawn
- pine trees
- lemon trees
- fig trees
- hedges
- hedges
- the vineyard
- the orchard

Revamped ground level

PROLOGUE

The first time I visited Italy was during one of the most difficult times in my life. A man I had known and loved, my boyfriend in college and later my first husband, died. To be precise, he killed himself.

His name was Phil, or to others, Philip. We had been together for ten years. We met when I was a wide-eyed college freshman, learning, for the first time, what it was like to live thousands of miles away from home and family on the campus of a large Midwestern university that was itself the size and population of a small city. Phil was the world-wise senior who taught me not only how to persevere in the blind maze of the registrar's office, but how to persevere in life. He was full of wisdom and could recite by heart the poetry of Keats and Blake. He taught me about ideals and persistence and perseverance in the face of hardship, until, it turned out, he could persevere no more.

I was devastated and disconsolate. In the months prior to my trip—a few months after his death—I spent most of my time in a zombie-like state in which I could do little more than weep quietly at my office desk. The shock of what had happened was too great. There was no note. There was no motive. He had not been depressed. I found out late one Friday morning, a day I had taken off from work, when two police officers rang my buzzer and asked to come in to talk. Before the buzzer sounded, I had been putting a load of wet laundry into the dryer and musing over what I might make for dinner. With the sound of a bell, my neat, orderly life lurched and shifted and twisted, wrung out like a sponge, never to be the same again.

And after that, it wasn't, and I wasn't.

"Why don't you take some time off?" my friend Marianne asked.

That summer, just a couple of months after the cops had come knocking at my door on that fateful day, Marianne had been the one to drag me out of bed, insisting that I sweat with her through aerobics class or join her for a concert or for dinner. Although I really wanted to stay in bed, I gave in to her nagging. Maybe listening to Marianne's love and work troubles was better than staying at home feeling sorry for myself. The summer passed this way, with Marianne and other friends making a point to invite me to dinner or a movie just to get me out of the house. For a time, I was counseled by the pastor who had presided over Phil's funeral, and after that, I visited a therapist for a short time. None of it made much of a difference. I was deeply depressed. Somehow, it didn't feel like I was living my own life anymore. I was living someone else's.

As summer turned to fall, colleagues at work returned from their summer vacations re-energized. I, however, sat blankly in front of my computer screen. Six months passed. Each new month was as gray and bleak and empty as the last. Seeing how things were going, Marianne one day took matters into her own hands. She marched into my editor's glass office and asked for something I had been unable to ask for myself.

"Please, *please* give Pam a leave of absence," she pleaded. "She can't go on like this. She's falling apart!"

And she was right. I spent most of my time, both at work and at home, in tears. On drives home from the office, alone in my car, I could let myself go full throttle. Sobbing while on the highway, I wondered what would happen if I rammed my car into a tree. I listened to a lot of Van Morrison, a favorite of Phil's. All the physiological workings of my body seemed to slow. Cell division had stopped. I was stuck like a lab specimen in a jar of formaldehyde. In a flash, I saw that life wasn't controllable. Nothing was safe and secure. Back in L.A., my parents, with their secure government jobs, weekly shopping rituals and general sense of industry, had provided me with a grand illusion of safety, a masterful feat in the late 60s and mid-70s with so much turmoil and strife unfolding in the world. There had been gas rationing, genocide in faraway countries, hostage-taking, war and whirring police helicopters right outside my door. My world, however, felt removed from all that, as soft and warm as the fleece pajamas I pulled on each night. Despite the bad news, it seemed to my child's mind that what happened in anyone's life, in the end, could largely be controlled and that life circumstances generally improved, as in the books I read and sit-coms I watched. I had accepted this illusion and thrived on it, right up until the doorbell rang that sunny April morning. But once the illusion was definitively torn and shredded to bits, I began to see that there was nothing to do but immerse myself in life's bewildering volatility. On some deep level, I recognized that, in this horror, there was an opportunity. This feeling was usually just a brief flicker, arising and dissolving quickly, but when it came, it was startling and electric. It was like getting a glimpse of something enormous and important, something that could ultimately change your life, but just for one maddening second, making it hard to understand what you had seen.

Sometimes, comfort and safety can anesthetize. But at age 26, standing before the corpse of my 30-year-old husband, I got a shock so strong I could do nothing other than wake up in a fit, from my comfortable old life. Nothing had prepared me for this. So why are we here? What happens when we die? Are our lives predestined? Phil had seemed to think so, taking his life, as his father had when Phil was a child.

I had always asked a lot of questions. My entire life, family and friends had teased that a conversation with me at times could feel like an interrogation. But now my mind stewed and chewed on all the big questions. I spent a lot of time on the phone with Phil's sister, trying to figure out exactly what had happened. We could guess that the fact that Phil's father had committed suicide when Phil was a child, and that Phil's mom was bipolar had something to do with it. Phil's brother and sister, themselves, had struggled with depression as a result. But I couldn't ruminate about these things while running from interview to interview. I needed time to think. I couldn't reconcile my life of a few months ago—a close connection with a partner who had cheered me through advanced biology exams in college, encouraged me to pursue internships and jobs no matter how far away, who ultimately uprooted his life to join me in Boston—I couldn't reconcile all that love and support with subsequent abandonment. Our nights at the dinner table discussing the events of the day, the afternoon phone calls to check-in while at work, weekend trips to the seashore with friends, I had thought those would be in my life forever. And yet, they had all dissipated as quickly as steam vapor on a bathroom mirror. And so, my editor, after twirling a lock of his hair for a few minutes as he did when he was in deep thought, kindly granted Marianne's request—a six-month leave of absence. I would use it to travel the world in my new emotional state—cracked wide open like an egg.

In October, I left. I first spent a couple of weeks with college friends in Fort Collins, Colorado, then flew to see my cousin in Sonoma, California, then on to my family in Los Angeles. I spent time among people who loved me, and did a lot of reading and thinking, immersing myself in books like M. Scott Peck's *The Road Less Traveled* and Alan Watt's *The Wisdom of Insecurity*. I felt plenty of insecurity. Might as well find some wisdom in it.

After visiting friends and family, I set off on my own to travel the world. I'm not sure where this idea came from. I only knew that I felt I had seen only a tiny corner of the fullness of existence. Now, not only did I want to process what had happened, but I wanted to experience all that fullness and not just remain an observer, as I had for so long as a reporter. Originally, I had wanted to go trekking in Nepal, but by the time I had been granted leave, it was the wrong season for that. So instead, I planned to visit Fiji, New Zealand, Australia, Hong Kong, Thailand, Italy, and finally Spain. My destinations were chosen partially based on the flight routes of the TWA open "round the world" ticket you could buy at the time. I was ready to embrace whatever I might find. For the first time in my life, divested of expectations or plans, I wanted to live life fully grounded in each vivid moment, as the Buddhist books I had been reading encouraged me to do. If living a full life meant going willingly into the unknown, of embracing uncertainty, I was there.

In this frame of mind, I eventually arrived in Italy, where I was to meet my friend Carolyn. I had already visited five countries, and while I can't say I had fully come to grips with the depths of my grief, somehow along the way, I had been reminded that there was a world still out there waiting for me, and that was hopeful. Carolyn and I planned to tour a corner of it together. Very early one morning in February, direct from Thailand, my plane touched down at Rome's Fiumicino Airport. Wearing a light cotton skirt and a sleeveless t-shirt that had been almost too heavy for the Thai heat, the first thing I noticed was how inadequate my clothing was. Italy that year was experiencing record cold. There was even a sprinkling of snow on the ground. And so, right there in the airport, before I did anything else, I dug through my dirty yellow tote and piled on every bit of clothing I had with me, topped by a leather jacket I had had made in a tailor's shop in Hong Kong.

When I got to the city, I met Carolyn at our designated meeting point—a small simple *pensione* in Rome's Jewish quarter, which we had rented thinking mostly of my slim budget.

"I can't believe we're here!" we exclaimed to each other gleefully when I was led up to Carolyn's room.

"Isn't it strange?" Carolyn said.

Once settled in, we set out to see the sites. We found a frigid city devoid of American tourists. They were afraid of traveling during the Gulf War, wary of possible terrorist attacks against Americans. That meant Carolyn, and I had the monuments, piazzas, and churches almost entirely to ourselves, as it was too cold to leave the house for most Italians who were used to much milder winter temperatures. We were ushered into the Sistine Chapel after only the briefest of waits. We strolled around the Roman Forum and freely snapped photos without other tourists wandering into the frame. We didn't even have to worry about Roman "guards" in full costume, pestering us for a photo. It was too cold for them to wander around wearing nothing but a skirt and a breastplate. In Piazza Navona, artists desperate for business offered to draw our portraits at a discount.

After just a few hours in Italy, I quickly recognized that something was different. Carolyn did too. Initially, we couldn't put a finger on it. Yes, the plates of pasta, pungent pizzas, and lush desserts were exquisite. My cappuccino arrived with a heart drawn in foam. Men turned their heads when I passed, but the looks were mostly cordial and respectful in contrast to the sinister catcalls I had gotten as a teen in South Central L.A. And yes, the centuries upon centuries of history packed tight into every conceivable corner was fascinating and extremely atmospheric.

"Notice the men," Carolyn remarked to me one afternoon near the Spanish Steps. "They're almost better looking than the women!"

And it was true. Both sexes were dressed with care, but the men in their well-fitting pressed pants and buffed loafers presented a stark contrast to most men I knew back in the States, who walked the streets in white sneakers, baggy acid-washed jeans, and baseball caps. (For them, dressing up meant switching to khaki pants.) But the men in Italy put me, in my Bangkok t-shirts and skirts, to shame. I could easily see that people in Italy knew how to live—indulgently, unrushed—in a way far superior to the way Americans lived. Life was about quality, not speed. We're all going to die anyway, what's the big rush in getting there? Let's live in style! There was something very Zen about it, as it required an appreciation of the nuances and intricacies of the present moment. In fact, it was Zenner than Zen, because Zen seemed like something you had to work at. But the Italians didn't have to work at anything. They just *were*. I soaked it all in, in my new state of awareness. But what was it that they knew?

The answer to that question, I was to find a few years later. This is the story of that discovery.

HOME # ONE
A *CASETTA* IN SARDINIA–
ZONA MAMUNTANAS

The first thing I noticed was the smell of something pungent. The fragrance was herby, like rosemary, or maybe lavender or thyme. It was full and rich and round, an aromatic confirmation that we had landed in some very different place. The sun shone brightly. The water was a beautiful shade of aqua and the sky a clear deep cerulean blue. Craggy rocks projected majestically out of serene waters, and we could hear the shrieks of seagulls. All the colors and odors and the bright sunshine pulsated in a way that felt hyperreal. It reminded me of how I felt one dazzling summer afternoon in the Berkshire Mountains after consuming psychedelic mushrooms. This time, though, no drugs were involved.

"This feels like a dream," I said to Umberto. "It doesn't feel real."

We had just disembarked in Sardinia after a punishing eight-hour ferry ride from the port city of Civitavecchia on mainland Italy. We had taken Umberto's family's battered

'87 Alfa Romeo and loaded it down with our black army bags and our big shaggy dog, Tony, who, panting optimistically, assumed we were taking him someplace fun. Of course, the ferry hadn't been much fun, particularly for the dog. As soon as we boarded, we were told that all dogs were to travel in metal cages on the lower level of the ferry. We reluctantly put Tony in one, before ourselves climbing to an upper level, to a darkened room of *"poltrone"* (or easy chairs) where we tried, in strange and uncomfortable positions, to get some sleep for the overnight trip. About midway through the ride, as the loud rumble of the ferry caused our chairs to vibrate, I felt the tap of a cold, wet nose on my leg.

"Tony!" I hissed, in a surprised whisper. Somehow, Tony had broken out of his prison, opening the door of his metal crate and roaming every floor of the enormous four-level ferry without being intercepted by the Italian ferry personnel. For the rest of the ferry ride, amazed and amused at his pertinacity, we kept Tony with us, hiding as best we could an 80-pound Newfoundland mix mutt whose head easily brushed our hips. Somehow, neither the drowsy passengers around us nor the indifferent ship stewards, seemed too concerned.

By morning, when the ferry slowly skimmed into port, we were tired but jubilant. Not only had we managed to evade any ferry authorities looking to imprison our dog, but we were about to embark on a whole new life, a whole new home, a whole new adventure.

It was early, just about 7 a.m. The sun was still low enough that the shadows of the Mediterranean scrub were still long. We had a two-hour drive to Torralba, the small interior village town where we were to stay.

We took Tony to a vacant lot near the shipyard and allowed him to attend to his needs while we surveyed, in the distance, the town of Olbia. The streets were lined with buildings in various peachy hues, but aside from the cars and people leaving the ship, there was hardly anyone visible on the sidewalks or roads.

"Where is everybody?" I asked Umberto.

We got back into the car and wended our way through town and then the countryside beyond. We drove on a pinched two-lane "highway" of knotted roads that looped and twisted through the Sardinian hills as large trucks hurtled past us at breakneck speed, setting my heart to pounding. After a long night on the ferry, another long ride felt tedious. I told Umberto to slow down because the hairpin turns were making me nauseous.

Snaking through rocky brush and cork trees, it began to dawn on me that, eerily, I had only seen a couple of grizzled old men in flat caps and a couple of elderly women draped in black shawls that flapped in the island breeze like bat wings. Other than that, I saw nothing but sheep.

There are moments in life that feel surreal. There are places and situations that go so far beyond your assumptions of life that they feel like scenes spun from a movie reel. You're watching life from the seat in the theatre, not performing on screen. That's what I felt now. This wasn't my life. My life was back in Boston, working as a reporter for *The Boston Globe*. And before that, back in Los Angeles, growing up in South Central L.A. Boston was about deadlines and interviews and office politics, triple-deckers, sometimes dilapidated, and the peculiar Boston accent that drops the "R." My life in South Central had been about police helicopters whirring overhead, pruned palm trees, gang rivalries, shopping malls, women in false eyelashes with long, wavy weaves tumbling down their backs, endless miles of pavement, and the rumble of cars roaring down L.A.'s 405 freeway. Umberto had led a different life too, and it hadn't involved swerving to avoid sheep in the road. Rather, it was about sidestepping roaring motor scooters in harrowing traffic circles and negotiating crowded piazzas christened with scrawls of colorful graffiti. In Umberto's world, tourists from every country clambered past ancient ruins surrounded by gangs of tattered gypsy children. Things, people, cars, whizzed by at full-tilt, and a bus ride across the city often concluded only after you were indecorously separated from your wallet. It was a street-wise kind of life, punctuated by a drag on a cigarette with your morning coffee. But this place couldn't be more alien from any of that. Here, we smelled the scent of rosemary in the air rather than car exhaust fumes. From the car window, we could glimpse sparkling blue waves that eventually gave way to lunar rocks and imposing cliffs. Here, there was purity.

How did I get here? It was the line out of The Talking Heads song *"Once in Lifetime,"* but in reverse.

Somehow, as a kid in L.A., then as a college student in Missouri, and finally as a big-city journalist in Boston toiling over reports on Betsey Johnson's latest collection, I had never imagined myself living among sheep, shepherds, and black-stockinged widows.

Yet here I was.

It would happen like this: I would fall in love with an Italian. I would leave my job at *The Boston Globe*. I would move to Italy. And upon arrival, I would take up residence not in one of the more storied and romantic Italian locales such as Rome, Milan or Florence, but instead in the remote hinterlands of the island of Sardinia—a long, grueling boat journey from the western coast of Italy. I would be moving to one of the poorest and least populated regions of Italy. I would encounter people and places that I couldn't have imagined, doing unfamiliar things in very strange ways. I would be pretty much the only African-American woman in an area of 9,000 square miles. There were no weaves here. No endless miles of pavement.

Had I lost my mind?

People who didn't know my whole story but who knew a thing or two about Sardinia, cautioned us about what we were getting into. "Moving to Sardinia, for Italians," said Alessandro, an Italian friend in his thick, staccato, over-enunciated accent, "is like moving to rural Iowa for a New Yorker." In other words, urbanites like Umberto and me, born and raised amid smog and traffic lights and people, people, people, might find ourselves adrift in a place so quiet that only the buzzing of weed-whackers and the distant tinkle of sheep bells penetrated a thick blanket of silence. Sardinia is large, isolated, and, worst of all, depending on your perspective, empty. Who went to live there?

A few friends of mine, I am sure, thought I was a fool for moving to a foreign country with a foreign man who undoubtedly had very foreign ideas about, among other things, committed relationships. Italian friends thought I was nuts for giving up a good job. But if there is one thing I had learned after the sudden death of my husband, it was that life was a risky proposition, whether I elected to take the risks myself or not. After nearly thirteen years as a newspaper reporter, I had arrived at a point where I was tired of my "observer" status. I had found myself in a lot of unlikely places—interviewing death row inmates inside the Louisiana State Penitentiary, gasping for fresh air during a forest fire at Yellowstone, marveling at a rocketing space shuttle at Cape Canaveral, perched alongside the catwalks of Paris fashion shows, interviewing all manner of author and actor, and designer and public official. I had recounted the stories of every sort of person in every station of life. But I was always the gawking, gaping onlooker. Now I wanted to be a protagonist in my own yet-to-be-written story. After years of reporting on what other people were doing in the world, I wanted to "do" something myself. It wasn't exactly a mid-life crisis, but maybe you could call it a quarter-life crisis. Just as this insistent longing grabbed hold, I met Umberto. And when he was offered a shot at a job as a researcher at a university in Sardinia, it didn't seem so farfetched to seize the opportunity to write a whole new story with him. It was a plucky move but a security-minded one, too. Now, we would build a life in a totally different place, new to both of us, while experiencing for ourselves a whole lot of things for the first time. I would speak a new language and live in a new culture, which was the adventure part. Umberto would launch an academic career, not an easy thing in Italy, where new grads are lucky to find even a short-term contract job after college. That was the security part. Would it be possible, I wondered, to reinvent myself like the intrepid and triumphant protagonist of some New York Times bestseller?

While at the newspaper, a joke circulated around the newsroom about life in "the velvet coffin." A job at the *Globe* was a job you had until death. The pay was decent, the company treated its employees well, life was comfortable. If an employee was reasonably good and did the job, there was no reason to expect that she wouldn't work there for 40 years before retiring with a comfortable pension. (Little did I know that the internet would come along to shred daily journalism as I knew it. It would get harder in the future to earn a living by words.) I had attended plenty of newsroom cake-and-coffee gatherings in honor of retiring colleagues who had done exactly this.

But unlike some of my colleagues, I wasn't ready for a life-long job at age 30, and I wasn't ready to be thinking about a secure retirement. I didn't want my future to be so well-planned that there was nothing to discover. There was too much out there. I had gotten a taste of it as a reporter, and glimpsed it again, in a different sort of way, as a grieving widow. If my old life at *The Globe* had been life in the velvet coffin, well, moving to Sardinia was maybe just one way to pry the lid off.

Sardinia is both large and small. Only about 1.65 million people live on the island but it is the second-largest Italian island after Sicily. Aside from the Italian coast and Sicily, the largest nearest land masses are Corsica to the north and Tunisia to the south. It is a treasured and traditional vacation haven for Italians, who, each August, descend on beaches boasting turquoise waters as clear as glass. They cavort and preen along with frisky dolphins, especially in areas like Costa Smeralda, made famous simply because celebrities tether their yachts there. Princess Diana visited just before her death. Bradley Cooper, Denzel Washington, and Lenny Kravitz have all visited. But Beyoncè and Elton John, sunning on sandy shores, taking dips in the pellucid sea, have no idea about "real life" Sardinia. Real-life Sardinia unfolds very slowly, in the crevices and folds of the hills in the center of the island. It is an entirely different reality. I hadn't read about it in any of the guidebooks I bought before coming. That part I hadn't read; it was something I was to discover.

And naturally, that's where we were headed.

We would be staying at the house of Francesca Piga, a long-time friend of Umberto's mother. Umberto's parents lived in Rome, as did this family friend. The house was Francesca's second home, empty most of the time, so she generously offered it to us as a place to stay until we could get our bearings. After all, she had no plans to be there until August, the one month of the year when Romans customarily exchange the city's blistering heat for the cool breezes of a seaside or mountain setting. The house, she thought, would be convenient for us. Torralba was located just south of Sassari where Umberto would be working.

We arrived by mid-morning, legs cramped from the drive. Tony bounded eagerly out of the small space between bags and boxes that we had managed to make for him in the car. Tongue dangling, tail wagging, he maintained a faith that we had brought him someplace fun.

The village house was of typical stone covered in stucco, a two-story structure attached to a series of similar houses lining the main street in the little hamlet of only about 1000 souls tucked into a bluff surrounded by desolate wind-swept plateaus, twisted cork trees and very short shepherds with bad teeth. The house seemed nearly as large as a department store, and in fact, included a storefront where decades ago the inhabitants had sold fruits and vegetables or, I imagined, maybe agricultural implements or supplies for livestock.

We unloaded. Even though we had sold off the contents of my apartment in Boston—a sagging couch with torn cushions went to an Albanian couple, my stone Buddha, heavy as a ship's anchor, had gone to my friend

Carla, a penny-pinching Russian had bought my paperbacks for five cents each after bargaining the price down from a sky-high 25 cents—we still had plenty of stuff with us. Our belongings included several huge black army bags, packed with everything imaginable and inessential, from silver trays to glass candlesticks to Haitian sculptures. It seems ridiculous, in retrospect, to travel the world with so many objects that I would later find to be expendable, but at that moment, each item represented security, the kind of safe and familiar trinkets that used to adorn my parent's large hi-fi console back in L.A. A psychiatrist might have called them transitional objects.

Improbably, we had even brought two kilim rugs that Umberto's brother graciously offered to transport as check-in luggage after a visit to Boston. Since I couldn't bear to part with many of my cherished, well-worn books, we boxed them up and mailed twelve boxes' worth to Italy. (Thanks to an international law on mailing literature, that I knew nothing about, that is, until Umberto told me about it, books could be mailed at a very low postal rate). The books hadn't yet arrived on the morning we settled in, but eventually, they would, causing a stir in Torralba's tiny post office.

The house was large, cold, and our voices echoed and reverberated through-out. With no soft surfaces, it felt institutional—like living in a hospital. There were many doors and many different hallways. Some hallways ran parallel to each other. We immediately decided to shut off an entire wing. "We don't need all this space to live, and we certainly don't need to heat it," said Umberto.

Straight away, I unpacked the colorful kilim rugs that had adorned my living and dining rooms in Boston. When we packed them, it had seemed a frivolous indulgence, but now in the cold and impersonal gloom of the village house, the bit of color and warmth they brought was appreciated. They reminded me of the home I had left behind while hinting at the new home we would try to create. And plus, we hadn't yet bought a dog bed, and the dog needed a soft place to lie down.

Those were our early days. Knowing neither people nor the language, I passed my days either attending Italian classes in Sassari, about 30 minutes away by car, or by burying myself in the books I had brought along with me. Italian classes at a small language school were the only fixed appointment in my very open schedule—my chance to immerse myself in negotiating the Italian language and culture without Umberto by my side. I used an international driver's license to get around, which technically was illegal—it was meant for tourists, not those, like me, overstaying their visas. (I would later rectify this problem by obtaining a stay permit.) Otherwise, you could find me reading in the courtyard behind the house, right next to the clothesline where our graying underwear was set out to dry. This is where I would often catch a glimpse of our next-door neighbor in the window, watching.

It was all so very different from Boston. When I met Umberto, I was living on the first floor of a brownstone building in Brookline. Although Brookline is technically a Boston suburb, it was close enough and interwoven enough into the fabric of Boston, to feel like just another city neighborhood. In fact, my apartment was so close to Fenway Park that though we couldn't hear the crack of the bat at game time, we would have trouble finding a parking spot on our street when the Red Sox were in town. I lived below Frank, a colleague of mine from *The Globe*, who lived with his partner Will in a smartly furnished home of beautiful antiques and vintage movie posters. They would throw parties from time to time and invite me up, and I would throw parties from time to time, and invite them down. I loved my life in Brookline. It was the convivial, semi-communal sort of life I had admired as a kid in the 70's watching Mary Richards with her pals Rhoda and Murray on *The Mary Tyler Moore Show*. I wanted to be like her—a career gal making her way in the big city. Like Mary Richards, I had several colleagues and friends who lived a short walk from my home. We would get together as regulars in our own style of newsroom sitcom. We threw Oscar parties, Sunday brunches, and birthday celebrations. It's what I had missed growing up in sprawling L.A., where people traveled miles in metal boxes on clogged roadways, just to see a familiar face. Boston was old and crumbling, tightly-woven and tight-knit. It sagged under the weight of history, but there was also a sense of community. L.A. felt rambling, rootless, uncentered and temporary. I didn't have many close friends growing up because all my schoolmates lived 20 miles away. Not only did I need a car, but I needed to be old enough to drive it.

In Boston, of course, I didn't worry about getting around. My friends lived in the neighborhood, and the party where I met Umberto was just a short walk from my apartment in Brookline. It was a late summer bash given by a friend of a friend of a friend, a chain so long that I didn't even know the name of the host. I invited my roommate Peter, who invited Carla, and she brought Umberto along. The night we met, we stood in a doorway inside a student crash pad on Beacon street, cradling red plastic beer cups, struggling to maintain a halting conversation in Spanish, the only language we both had in common.

"*Cuanto tiempo en Boston?*" I hazarded in the few words of Spanish I could remember from high school.

"*Come?*" responded Umberto in Italian.

That was about as far as it got. Of course, it wasn't so much that words mattered. Umberto had looked at me with his curious brown eyes, seemingly tantalized to be speaking with a foreign woman. I had returned his gaze, intrigued. It was party chatter, a simple flirtation set to UB40's *(I Can't Help) Falling in Love*. I had no idea at the time that this absurd, nonsensical conversation would shape the contours of my life for the next 20 odd years. I learned that Umberto was a Ph.D. student, finishing his doctoral dissertation during a six-month research stint at Boston University. He'd been in the country for only three months. He was reading *The Tao of Physics*, just like me, and he didn't smoke. I'm not sure when I learned all this, but it most certainly wasn't during our broken conversation that night. Still, I was motivated to press on, as Umberto was tall and handsome with a broad forehead and soulful brown eyes. If I couldn't talk to him, at least I could look at him.

After that night, we went on a few "dates," if you could call them that. They were Italian-style, which meant we went out with large groups of people, most of whom were visiting Italian doctoral students. It was the first thing I noticed—Italians move in groups. After a group date at a Chinese restaurant, then a group dance to a downtown discotheque, followed by a group visit to my home, I finally, in frustration, called Carla.

"Tell Umberto that if he likes me, we should make plans to see each other alone," I said. Carla passed this on. A day or two later, I got a phone call from Umberto.

"I am Umberto," he announced with authority.

Finally, we began to see each other in earnest, sans the supporting cast. I thought our brief romance was a fling—one of those dalliances women crave with men with foreign accents. I knew that, shortly, Umberto would return to Italy, and then it would all be over. Still, it was a wonderful change of pace from my very last relationship with a shaggy-haired bass musician I had met after Philip's death, and I managed to enjoy it for what it was. What I remember most about those days is that I had a perpetual smile plastered on my face. I beamed as I wrote stories on my newsroom computer monitor and I beamed as I inched through traffic on my way home from the office. I laughed while I showered each morning and giggled as I poked and prodded melons and squash while grocery shopping. I wore a broad smile when I took Tony out for walks, no matter how brisk the temperature or how stinging the pelting rain. My neighbors must have thought I was an extraordinarily friendly woman.

Then Umberto left.

But about a month or two after Umberto left the country, to my surprise, he did return. He moved in with me, and Peter moved out. Tony made room for the interloper in my life, although not before chewing his socks to fine bits the first night he slept over, just to show who was boss. Umberto's English slowly improved while I took a short course in Italian where, serendipitously, it turned out that my teacher hailed from the Sardinian town of Iglesias.

In those first heady months living in my brownstone apartment together, while Umberto wrote his dissertation and I covered fashion shows for *The Globe*, Umberto had "an opportunity" in Sardinia. I use quotes, because it was nothing more than that. It wasn't a firm job or even a job offer. It was a chance to apply for a job at a medium-sized university in the island's second largest city of about 200,000 residents, if you stretched to include the surrounding townships. Since the university was founded in 1562, there was even a small bit of cachet attached.

"How would you feel about moving to Sardinia?" he asked me one day.

"Where is Sardinia?" I responded.

Maybe once in my life I had heard someone mention Sardinia. But it was only once. I didn't know where it was located or what life could be like there. Umberto showed me a map and described how beautiful it was based on a short camping trip he had once taken. It sounded pleasantly exotic. I began to take a fancy to the idea of it based on his limited experience of the place. For a person like me, who, before my first husband's death, had always done the right things, and been totally immersed in career, it meant coloring outside the lines. And when I had visited Italy a couple of years earlier, I had loved it. I came to relish the idea of creating a new sort of home in a totally new, very exotic place. Plus, Umberto was great at whipping up enthusiasm. He was that type of guy—optimistic, action-oriented. He didn't read a lot of books, which frustrated me, (I don't think he even read *The Tao of Physics*—it had only been a stab at impressing me) but he was always out *doing* things. Now we could do something entirely new together. On the other hand, if this didn't work out, if I arrived in Sardinia and found I didn't like it, I would have relinquished a good job, a great apartment, good friends, for… what, exactly?

In Boston I had spent a lot of time making my brownstone rental feel homey, but in Torralba the set-up both inside and outside the house was less inviting. In

Boston, I surrounded myself with vintage furniture, my own watercolors, old hand-me-down paintings, and Indian textiles draped artfully over my torn sofa. I painted a niche in the living room a bright coral, and my study a mint green. It was a little bit bohemian with a creative, ever-so-slightly intellectual air. But that wasn't the feeling around me now. Everything felt utilitarian and serviceable, and most of it was in service of agriculture. In the village, if you did not own a flock of sheep, there was very little to do. And when it came to leisure activities, there were none of the city amusements I enjoyed in Boston. There were no bookstores to hang out in, no afternoon matinees to catch, no window-shopping. I didn't mind, though. After the daily grind of working at a newspaper for more than a decade which followed directly after college, taking leisurely walks in the country and reading and thinking on my own was enough for me. And plus, although I had friends back in Boston, I was essentially an introvert, always content with a good novel over people. Books didn't tease and torment, no matter how fat you were, or how thick your glasses. Now I was tall and slim and wore contact lenses instead of coke-bottle lenses, but I still felt awkward around people unless I switched into reporter's mode where I could ask a lot of questions to keep the attention off myself. I was comfortable being left to my own devices. As quiet as my days were, I still felt liberated.

Once a week, traveling vendors caravanned into town to form an outdoor market in the local soccer field, where villagers bought kitchen utensils, socks or perhaps a pair of house slippers. They lined their trailers up and sold whatever they had to offer to townspeople who they knew by name. That too, was a contrast with how I grew up. Back in L.A., my mother took us shopping at the popular discount store Gemco, where she would buy a large cart's worth of groceries, clothing, and packages of Mrs. Field's chocolate chip cookies for us to scarf down on the ride home. In the village, there were none of these large discount stores. People lived mostly the way they always had, except now the market vendors sold Chinese imports and shepherds guided their flocks through grassy pastures from the comfort of their cars rather than on foot or by horse.

Whenever I left the house, I had a strange feeling of being transported out of time. In some ways, I felt like I was living the way my grandparents had lived in what I had seen as a child in the rural American South. People grew their own vegetables. Corner shops were small and sold local produce. Everyone greeted each other on the street and people, as a sign of respect, uttered salutations using professional titles. *"Buon giorno professore!" "Buon giorno ingegnere!"* In Boston, nobody even took the time to say hello, much less attaching an honorific to the greeting. And in South Central L.A., the greeting that made the biggest impression on me was the hand signals thrown between gang members.

From the moment we arrived in Torralba, two giants in the land of very petite people, everyone in the village seemed to already know our names. Word spreads quickly in the *paese*.

Late one morning, a diminutive smiling woman appeared on our doorstep. She wore sensible Sardinian shoes and a severe straight skirt that reached to mid-calf.

"Paaa-maay-laaaa?" I heard her call.

Umberto had left for the university, where he was preparing for a *concorso* for the job he didn't actually have yet. But I was home, engrossed as usual, in a book. When I answered the door, a small woman with hair dyed an unlikely shade of eggplant, uttered a torrent of words in Italian while shoving a carefully wrapped flat package into my arms. I didn't know her, but somehow, she seemed to know me, and from what I could make out, she knew a lot about Umberto, the details of his job and his schedule. Certainly, she knew Francesca, and even something about Umberto's mother. I took the wrapped package, surprised.

"*Grazie, grazie tanto*," I said.

I wanted to do something, invite her in for coffee at least to exchange a few words, but at this point, I had no words to give. If she had come in to sit in our little windowless *salotto*, I would only be able to nod and smile blankly, like a foreign fool.

Understanding that I was catching little of what she said, she smiled and waved her hand as she turned away.

"*Mi raccomando, fammi sapere se hai bisogno di qualcosa*," she said, before pattering back down the street.

She wasn't the only villager to appear at our door in those earliest days. Sometimes they brought sweets, sometimes liquor. I always felt a mild sense of guilt; I wasn't used to such hospitality and didn't know how to respond. Being shy to begin with, my mangled Italian meant I couldn't even switch into reporter's mode. We would invite them in to sip their grappa or *filu 'e ferru* ("iron wire" in Sardinian dialect, referring to a time earlier in Sardinian history when moonshiners would hide their bootleg liquor in the earth, only detectable by a slim iron wire poking above the soil.) The liquor was so strong I concluded that it had been named iron wire because that's what it felt like as it hot pokered its way down my throat.

There were many appearances from all sorts. Mario, the shepherd who lived across the way, brought fresh milk that had come straight from the cow.

"Be sure to boil it first!" he warned us.

He invited us to see the new house he and Anna, his pregnant bride, were having built at the edge of the village. Unlike his small and damp village house, built centuries ago, his new villa was to be filled with all the modern conveniences. It would have a dishwasher and a large yard, and it would get sun in the mornings. It would not be damp and humid, like the old village houses.

In the afternoons, Anna would visit and tell stories of the wedding she and Mario had thrown for 400 of Torralba's residents. I tried to imagine how much it might cost to throw a 20 course mega-feast for almost half the village. I visited her once or twice, but there were so many gifts stacked around their tiny living room there was never a place to sit. And then too, as much as I liked her, Anna and I had so little in common. Anna's script seemed bound by the village—marriage and children (not necessarily in that order), home and family. I, on the other hand, felt cold chills at the thought of having kids. For me, it represented restriction and confinement. It would permanently shift my life into an experience of the known—baby's first steps, swimming lessons, soccer clubs, college graduation—rather than an exploration of the unknown. Somehow, I didn't feel ready for that kind of certainty.

Giovanna, who lived on the other side of the street, would drop by on Sundays, proffering information about nearby archaeological sites we might visit. She, her mother and her aunt, a house full of women as many Sardinian houses seem to be, became our resource whenever we needed something. And we often did—advice on where to find certain housewares, where to find good pizza in the next village, which auto mechanic was the most reliable.

We were touched by the generosity of everyone in Torralba, but our brief time in the village revealed that we were far too attached to the diversity and relative openness of a city to disappear into the island's forbidden interior where life had remained unchanged for centuries. Despite all the polite ministrations, all the Sardinian cookies, fennel pulled fresh out of the ground, glasses of homemade *grappa* and *mirto*, we felt ourselves to be woefully out of place. Somehow, I had forgotten about the down side of small town life. On the other side of all that caring and closeness comes monitoring and surveillance. Coming from the city where no one took note of your presence unless you'd elected to walk the sidewalks nude, it was uncomfortable to be examined and dissected like a frog in a 7th grade science class. Though everyone was kind and gracious, I still felt like a frog.

I felt this more strongly than Umberto, since I was the sole resident of color in the tiny village. Evidently, a Moroccan man had once lived in Torralba. Villagers told stories. But it was so long ago, no one seemed to recall exactly when. That was about it for diversity. As a black woman, this was hard for me. I was used to being surrounded by people with much paler skin tones than my own. I had been bussed to junior high and high school in a predominately white, wealthy neighborhood of Los Angeles, before attending college at a large, predominately white, Midwestern college. The majority of my boyfriends had been white, as had been Philip, and most of my friends. Still, I came from a culture in which African-Americans were an integral, accepted fact, even among those who may have preferred otherwise. Here, blacks were exotic and foreign, and I stood out in a way that grew tiresome. At least in Rome, the Italians had seen enough foreign tourists to take skin color differences in stride. But in 1996, Sardinians had not seen many people of color. When villagers saw black women, they often assumed they were prostitutes, since a good number of the streetwalkers lining the tissue-strewn backroads at night were African.

One late afternoon, when I left the village house to take Tony on a walk, I strolled down the hushed main street beyond the village, just reaching the outskirts of town where the road continued along empty mountain pastures. As I passed the last pizza restaurant and then the town soccer field, an ancient toothless shepherd, probably in his 70s, wearing the usual flat cap, pulled up beside me in a creaky old sedan to offer me 40,000 lire (or about $23) if I would disappear with him down some country lane to do unspeakable things.

"I am not a prostitute!" I exclaimed in Italian, shocked. I wished I spoke better Italian so that I could hurl more cutting insults. To impress upon him just how loutish he had been, I added in my limited Italian: "I am the wife of a professor!" (Italians have a lot of respect for professors although I was of course stretching the truth—Umberto and I weren't married yet and Umberto was still working on that first step of becoming a researcher—it was an aspirational retort.)

"Well then," responded the toothless old shepherd, "how about 100,000 lire?"

I needed to be on the coast, where tourists spoke different languages, and where different skin colors passed through from time to time, where life felt less insular. In some sense, we wanted to recreate the freedom that anonymity brings in a city.

Umberto felt this too, even though he was Italian and thus more familiar with Italian village ways. Though he knew what a village felt like for a few weeks at a time based on summer vacations at his parent's small hometown village in Abruzzo, he was still the citified son of an oil company executive and a government worker. Living in a village had sounded quaint to both of us, but we were experiencing its limitations.

One morning on which we were planning a short trip back to the mainland, Umberto took Tony out for a walk especially early. It was about 5:30 a.m. and the sun wasn't up yet. Our next-door neighbor, however, was up, and already leaning against the facade of his house like a loyal prison guard on assignment. He spent all day, every day, just like this. And now we knew, he also spent all night too.

"*Un po' presto stamattina!*" (A little early this morning!") he remarked to Umberto.

The afternoon I "disappeared" made our fishbowl status even more apparent. As always on my afternoon walk with big, bounding Tony, I left the house before the sun dropped too low in the sky, pulling shut the heavy wooden door that groaned with a loud echo that reverberated up and down Torralba's one main street. I crossed the main road and headed for a nearby well-trodden dirt path established by shepherds, which meandered back into the hills, probably for many miles. I only did a part of it—the usual route I took before doubling back to the village. As usual, I passed a sun-creased villager, age 80 or maybe even 90, out doing the backbreaking work of hoeing and pulling weeds.

That night, when Umberto returned home, the lights were on, but the house was empty. I didn't leave a note because I was not expecting to be gone for very long. And besides, this wasn't Boston or even L.A. I would not be caught in a gang shoot-out between the Crips and the Bloods. Panicking in this era before cell phones, Umberto wandered the village asking random townspeople if they had seen me. Everyone, it turned out, had an answer. One village elder who spent most of his day roosted on a chair in front of his house, reported that I had left the house at approximately 4:40 p.m., my usual time. Another woman a few doors down observed that she had seen me walk by at about 4:45 p.m., as usual. Still another could verify that I had passed at about 5:10. p.m. With frightening ease, Umberto could establish a decisive timeline in which every villager had seen and noted my presence on the street. Certainly I, standing 5'10, with long dreadlocks cascading down my back, stood out from the very short villagers. As it happened, Giovanna had invited me and the dog in for tea and cookies, and that's where I was. As I made polite conversation in my impaired Italian and munched on *ciambelline*—flaky little confections filled with jam—and *pabassinas*, nutty raisin cookies filled with almonds and walnuts, Umberto rang the bell. With very little detective work, he had traced the exact route of my walk right up to the scrubbed concrete steps of our neighbor's house directly on the other side of the road.

"There you are!" he said with relief. After we got back home, he admonished me: "Why didn't you leave me a note?"

Later, with amusement, we marveled that my daily activities had been monitored by practically every eye in the village. It was charming and sweet, but it was also kind of scary.

Beginning our housing search with a few months of island life under our belts, we realized we were luckier than many couples looking for a new home. Although Umberto and I were born and raised in different cultures speaking different languages, we somehow clung to the same vision about at least this one thing.

"Where would you like to live?" I asked him one evening over a heaping plate of pasta. We could think about these things, now that he had won his *concorso*. He was now a researcher and safely on an academic track, so we were free to dream. It was the same conversation we had almost every night, but we never tired of repeating it. Who knew that once we learned each other's language, it would turn out that we would use only a few phrases? We were settled around a small table in our windowless *salotto*, one of the many internal rooms in Francesca Piga's Torralba house. The TV blared a laugh track from "*Striscia la Notizia*," (translating roughly as "The News Comic Strip"), an Italian satirical news show airing every night around dinner time.

"Well," he responded, "it needs to be near a highway so that I can get to the university, but I really don't see the point of living in a city in Sardinia," he continued. "If the best thing the island has to offer is its natural beauty, why should we go live in a mediocre town?"

He had no argument from me. Why move to Sardinia, only to be marooned in one of its drab, cinder block villages? A village made sense for villagers born and raised in a village. It made less sense to outsiders with freedom of choice, like us. Village life, frankly, could be claustrophobic. On the other hand, I knew for myself that I did not want to be too far from civilization. We were both city folk, after all, and we needed to be near *something*. If we didn't expect to get milk directly from the cow, we wanted to be able to find a half-liter of milk in a store nearby.

"I agree," I told him, between bites of eggplant pasta. "I want to live on the outskirts of a small to mid-size town, but not in a village. I don't want anything big or fancy. Just a little bit of land, and something with some character."

We sliced two wedges of pecorino cheese and slipped it into our mouths, enjoying a moment of unity, always an occasion to be savored, I would later learn, in our long relationship.

My vision had undoubtedly been informed by my own childhood. Although I had lived in a rough neighborhood early on, it was essentially middle and working class. My parents owned a neat stucco bungalow—"*On the Edge of Watts*" we called it, joking that it could be the name of a new black soap opera airing after *The Edge of Night*—with a patch of lawn that my father mowed religiously every Saturday. I had also been influenced by the romantic reverie of books like *Under the Tuscan Sun,* which had come out the year we moved. I pictured the poor man's version—a simple stucco cottage, a beautiful garden, a guest house, a riot of pink and red geraniums under palm trees. I didn't use the word "adorable" with Umberto, but that's what I had in mind. In turn, he never used the word "*delizioso*" with me, but that's how it would have translated. Umberto had grown up in a large elegant apartment block with a *portiere*, or doorman, on the outskirts of central Rome. Strangely, his family occupied almost exactly the same socio-economic status as mine—his parents had clawed their way up from the working class into the middle-class in the 60s while supporting four children at the same time. His parents, like mine, had embraced the jobs, housing and amenities of the big city, despite their country roots. Now both of us seemed to be rebelling against the city, seeking our own romanticized, though sanitized, version of rural life. The thought of renting never crossed our minds.

There was but no question that we would buy a piece of property together. We were looking for something we could mold and shape the way we saw fit. We were looking to recreate a piece of ourselves in our own image, and we wanted to do it without needing to ask a landlord for permission. I had built up savings from my years of work at *The Globe*, and Umberto's father was offering each of his sons help in buying a house, so we didn't even need a mortgage. Plus, owning rather than renting was a sign of commitment. In owning, we were rooting ourselves to Sardinia and to each other in the same way that having children roots couples to each other, and to a place. This common vision bound us together even in the face of a different, decidedly less picturesque reality.

That is, Sardinia's constructed environment was not always so pretty, often because of the Sardinian's individualist streak. Sardinians are a people used to going it alone. Undoubtedly this is a result of a pastoral history in which shepherds would ascend, along with their sheep, deep into the hills for months at a time. Most likely, this is the origin of the "*Mamunthones*" figure, the mythical and frightening half man/half beast masked creature, sheathed in matted sheep fur and cowbells, that is a staple of Sardinian parades and festivals. I remember the first time I saw one at a parade held in Torralba's main square.

The loping, horned savage creature, cowbells straining around the neck, gave me nightmares for weeks. According to Sardinian legend, shepherds, living isolated among their sheep became themselves part man and part beast. And if there is anything to this, perhaps some of it can be seen in recent Sardinian history. There is a rough edge to Sardinian culture that includes violence and banditry. (Between 1966 and 1968, Sardinian bandits kidnapped 33 people, including one 14-year-old boy who they held captive in the hollow of a large tree. At the time that we arrived on the island, the kidnapping of Silvia Melis, daughter of engineer Tito Melis, was in the news.) In a historically subsistence economy based on raising sheep, tending to olive trees and squeezing sweet liquid from grapes, life is simple and austere. This pastoral existence means that Sardinia is significantly poorer than Italy's wealthier northern manufacturing regions. Even so, a temperate climate has meant that, compared to other societies in harsher climes, there is not much impetus to organize collectively in response to shared problems. Families help each other, friends help each other, but Sardinia is essentially an island of individuals, and each individual is quietly, stoically, going his own way.

This meant that the landscape was filled with individual solutions, as we were to see.

One afternoon on a house-hunting quest, we gingerly eased our car down a dusty, pitted road in an area near the university where Umberto worked. The ruts were so deep, they formed impressive canyons in the street, but a resourceful local, most likely someone in the construction trade, had decided to take care of the problem by filling the crevices with heaps of jagged tiles. As we drove over the makeshift solution, we heard a menacing pop.

"What was that?" I asked Umberto.

We looked at each other. Did this mean several hours stuck on this road, tending to a punctured tire? We had no cell phones to bail us out. We got out and peered at the dust-caked tires. Umberto, who had majored in engineering at the university, stuck his head under the car frame.

"It's okay, it's okay," he said, climbing back into the car. "It was the *ammortizzatore*."

Fortunately, the sharp snap we had heard was just the last gasp of our beleaguered shock absorbers. Continuing on, we noticed a distinct lack of "official" signs. The signs we saw were simple posts hand-painted by residents. Around a bend, behind a grove of trees, our car slid past a mountain of old washing machines, tires, broken-down refrigerators, and ragged couches. Apparently, the locals preferred their own makeshift neighborhood dump to the official town dump a few kilometers away. We drove past more than a few gates concocted of jerry-rigged mattress springs. They were ghastly to look at, but they served a purpose. Beyond the rusted, coiled gates stood houses that had never received the benediction of paint. A peculiarity of the Italian tax law declares a house to be "finished" only when that last coat of paint graces the facade. In order to avoid paying taxes on a "residence," many forgo painting altogether, content to live in grayed, somewhat forlorn houses. We rode through a landscape of abandoned dreams, cinder block skeletal frames of houses on which construction had begun but never ended. They spread out over the hillsides like animal carcasses.

By the end of the day, I was exhausted. All the jostling and bouncing around on the rough roads made me feel sore and achy as if I had been riding a horse. In fact, house-hunting by horseback would have been easier. But Umberto being Umberto, always pushing ahead for a new discovery, that one road that would change our lives, kept pressing the protesting car ahead, even as the sun began to slip below the prickly pear bushes lining the lane.

"Let's just try this road," he said as we bounced down one more street that he promised would be the last.

A few more excursions like this and we quickly began to see that Sardinia's man-made structures were not quaint in the way most tourists might imagine. While the Sardinian natural world is quite beautiful, recalling something of the California coastline, Sardinia didn't have the castle-and-moat fairy tale quality that Tuscany had. There were no manors, no rolling hills dotted with cypress trees, no undulating vineyards that were part of the vast estates of nobles. Some of it, in fact, reminded me of some of the more impoverished sections of Watts back in L.A.— the squat little cinder block houses, trash tossed carelessly in back alleys and on dead end streets. Problem is, of course, that we had Tuscany in our heads. Would we really be able to find a home in this new land, or was it too dramatic a change from what we both knew?

Each week, we bought a copy of *"L'Occasione"* (or The Deal), an island-wide magazine printed on stiff white paper consisting solely of classified ads offering cars, livestock, businesses, and even houses for sale. There was even a personals section for Sardinians seeking love, although it's hard to imagine the weathered Sardinians I'd met choosing to date this way. Each week the masthead changed colors so you could distinguish one week from the next. We pored over *L'Occasione* as if it were the map leading to the Holy Grail. After many long exploratory drives around the island, we decided we wanted to be near the coastal town of Alghero, about a half an hour drive west of Sassari. Alghero is an evocative small town of about 44,000 people, by turns beguiling and romantic. It has Spanish bastions overlooking craggy beaches suggesting the majestic sweep of history. It also has neighborhoods beyond the charming historic center consisting of weed-filled vacant lots. Founded in the twelfth century by the Genoese family of the Doria, Alghero was forced to surrender to a long assault of the Aragonesians in 1353. The Catalans arrived afterward, and to this day, the *Algherese* speak *"algueres,"* a dialect based on Catalan that is quite different from the Sardinian language and also quite different from Italian. What I liked about Alghero was a feeling it gave me of openness, something quite different from the atmosphere of Sardinia's interior. These coast dwellers were used to outsiders. We diligently circled possibilities in our dog-eared *L'Occasione* and set out on more long rides down chalky *strade bianche*, in search of "the one."

After weeks of looking, it began to dawn on us that we had no choice. We had seen only a handful of houses, and none came anywhere close to the gauzy beatific dream floating through our heads. (There was one that did, built to look like one of the prehistoric Nuraghe ruins around the island, but that was far out of our price range.) The layouts were consistently awkward. The interiors were consistently dark. The materials used for construction were consistently *"povera"* as the Italians might say. Where was the house with *"finiture di pregio"*? Where was the *"villa rifinitissima"*? Where were the potted geraniums and palm trees? *Delizioso*? Forget about it.

It was beginning to occur to me that what I wanted, and what Sardinia had to offer might be out of sync.

One problem was that, in that era, no one on the island opted to live full-time in what was referred to as *la campagna*. Despite the rural, pastoral flavor of the island, most Sardinians lived in densely-packed small towns or cities. It was not unusual to own a spacious apartment or house in the *"paese"* (or town) and then a *"campagna"* or little place two or three kilometers out of town for making wine, cultivating olives and growing vegetables. It is this tie to the land, which most every family has, which is probably responsible for the Sardinian earthy practicality and sensible and direct solutions found without a lot of unnecessary flourishes. The *campagna* can be just a little plot of land, or it can sometimes encompass many hectares. Usually there is a structure involved, often a simple concrete block box. This is where Sunday afternoon barbecues of *porceddu* (roasted pig on a spit) are held and where large and extended Sardinian families gather in the summer to sing karaoke off-key, deep into the night. Sardinians might choose to spend a weekend in their country house, or maybe even a week or two in August. But when the summer ends and the Mediterranean waters begin to cool, Sardinians quickly retreat to the reassurance of town, where they can once again meet friends for an espresso in the corner bar and walk along the *lungomare* after dinner. Old men in their caps gather at sidewalk tables where they can nurse an early-morning beer until early afternoon. There is safety and comfort in numbers.

Even Umberto's mother, usually approving of most everything her sons did, couldn't understand our fascination with the countryside. She had spent a few years of her youth in Sardinia and knew what was—and wasn't—out there.

"*Ma perche?*" she asked, pinching her fingers together in that characteristic Italian gesture. "*Perche?*"

Or, in other words, *why?*

Another week passed. We stopped once again at the corner *edicola* for the latest edition of L'*Occasione*. In the evening, over dinner, we opened it up in our damp little *salotto*. Again, "*Striscia la Notizia*," with its dancing showgirls and irritating purple puppet, blared on TV. (One of the lithe, smiling showgirls was Elisabetta Canalis, the Sardinian who would briefly and unsuccessfully attempt to maneuver George Clooney to the wedding altar before settling for an American orthopedic surgeon she would end up marrying in 2014.) We were eating pasta yet again. (It was cheap and easy to prepare, and at this time in our lives, our metabolisms were young and fast enough to handle it.) That week, the masthead of *L'Occasione* was an optimistic orange. That was promising. One ad caught our eye. It was a "villa" on about 5,000 square meters of land—or about one and a quarter acres. It was a couple of kilometers outside the town of Alghero on the island's northwest coast. The house came with a vineyard. The location was the right one. It sounded more than just promising. It sounded like it could be "the one."

"Let's go see it!" I exclaimed to Umberto.

"*Subito*!" he responded.

We were both excited. The next morning, we called the realtor and arranged a meeting.

The road to get there was, as usual, rough and dusty, dimpled with deep-set ruts and grooves. Invariably, a car would pull out on the street ahead of us, blasting a forceful cloud of powdery silt onto our car, and into our own car's ventilation system. The chassis of our old Alfa Romeo squeaked in protest. We choked and coughed. My eyes watered as dust settled under my contact lenses. Where *was* this house? After a while, we finally turned down a smaller dirt lane just off the main dirt road. At the end of the lane was a green gate surrounded by bougainvillea vines draped over pink stucco walls.

"It has to be this one," Umberto remarked.

The gate was open. A man leaned against the hood of a car in the driveway. Greeting us was Angelo, lean and brusque, who suspiciously, sized us up. Angelo was the caretaker for the homeowners, the Martellis, who, it turned out, lived in Tuscany.

We got out of our car and, feeling somewhat encouraged, followed Angelo and the realtor around the property.

The "villa" was little more than a storage shed where the original owners, three sisters, came to pick grapes and crush them into a particularly strong homemade version of the island's famous Cannonau wine. The three sisters had divided their property into three plots of land and sold them off piecemeal over time. "Our" plot had belonged to one of the sisters. It originally consisted of a one-room concrete shed with a cantina, a large garden, and a vineyard. The shed became a very small house when it was expanded by a couple more rooms over time to allow for a kitchen, a bedroom, a bathroom and a huge veranda large enough to act as the setting for Sunday afternoon barbecues. While the house itself measured only about 800 square feet, the veranda was very nearly the same size. All of it was later sold to the Tuscan family who, wielding their Tuscan magic, decided to shape the plot into a vacation paradise. They added a covered carport, planted palm trees, sodded an expansive lawn, painted the house pink, and imported dark, walnut furniture sturdy enough to take a beating from the hordes of family and friends who inevitably came to visit each summer.

The long fingers of a bougainvillea vine gracefully draped over one side of the veranda. Inside, the house was laid out in "farmhouse" style—that is, the front door opened directly onto a rustic kitchen of dark cabinets with dark brown floor tiles. Off this main room were three other small rooms, each with a different color tile. Although one was set up as a *"salotto"* or living room, it could also function as a bedroom. The entire house came completely furnished with heavy, pine furniture vaguely Alpine in style, adorned with blue floral cushions and matching blue floral curtains. It was all a bit old-fashioned for our taste, but since we didn't have any furniture, we weren't going to complain about it.

Of course, no one had ever lived here year-round. It was not even built for it. There was no real foundation. The one that existed would move slowly over the years like a sleeping giant shifting position in bed. We would later be required to shore it up, but we didn't know that at the time. The windows were thin, made of only one slight pane of glass that rattled whenever we opened and closed them. The concrete block structure was not insulated, nor built in the modern way that creates a double-layered wall to discourage the dampness that is a perpetual problem in old Sardinian houses. Stucco flaked off the damp concrete blocks both inside and out. We noticed this, but we didn't let it bother us.

Angelo threw open the doors and shutters, room by room, while we followed the trail of light. Umberto, as usual, bounded in first. I, more tentative, lagged behind.

Admittedly, the house was very, very dark, even when all windows were open, partly because it had only one real exposure. It shared a wall with a house attached on the north side. And that house was owned by one of the original three sisters. That meant dim sunshine filtered in from windows on mainly just one side. It faced south, but most of the light was purloined by the large veranda running the entire length of the house.

Still, there was something homey and reassuring about the luster of the dark wooden kitchen cabinets in the cozy gloom. What really set the house apart was its large, well-tended garden. Thanks to Angelo, it included a huge lawn that looked almost as pristine as a golf course, interspersed with fledgling pine trees, laurel and oleander bushes, surrounded by a neatly-trimmed hedge for privacy. In one corner of the lawn, Angelo had created a vegetable garden that he used to feed his rabbits, wherever they were. And beyond that stood a vineyard and even beyond that, an orchard of pear and plum trees. There was a myrtle bush from which Angelo made *"mirto,"* the sweet liquor that is brought out after every extravagant Sardinia meal. There were lemon trees, too, and of course, Angelo made homemade limoncello using their fruit. We could too if we bought the house. Even more significant for us were the palm trees and geraniums in fat terra cotta pots. Angelo and his wife had planted the geraniums with loving care. Strangely, all of it—the geraniums and palm trees, the lawn and pink stucco walls, the modest but still adorable dimensions of the house—were almost exactly what we had been envisioning. It was as if a genie had granted us our most fervent desire. Yes, it was humble and unpretentious, it was simple and unassuming, but it was also, well...*delizioso*. It was the romanticized version of "country" we had clung to all these months. Angelo skeptically led us to the perimeter of the property and showed us where the well and the septic tank were located. He also showed us how the irrigation tubes were set up to bring water to all four corners of the property. We could tell by his hardened, weather-beaten face, the raised eyebrows, his silences, the way he locked and unlocked doors, that he was dubious that these two city slickers could handle such a place. (Or perhaps he was simply in disbelief that anyone would be willing to pay good money for what was essentially a shack.) He even seemed a little sullen, angry perhaps, that he would no longer be able to grow vegetables and make wine and hold big Sunday afternoon gatherings on the veranda with his family while the Martellis were stuck trying to pay for it all at work back in Tuscany.

We got back into our car, excited.

"What do you think?" Umberto asked.

"I can't believe it," I marveled. "It's incredible how much it's exactly what I had in mind, right down to the terra cotta pots and geraniums. It's even furnished, and we have no furniture! It feels almost like magic."

"I know, I know," Umberto agreed. "It really *is* incredible!"

If New Age books and motivational speakers talk about "manifesting," we had apparently done a really great job of it here in Sardinia, where being able to manifest anything so specific seemed all the more unlikely.

On a day that happened to correspond to Thanksgiving in the United States, we sat down with the Martellis for a sumptuous and extended feast at a nearby restaurant, da Bruno (or Bruno's Place), known for the quality of its fish. Neither of us had fish, though. The Martellis ordered quail. We tried the *cinghiale*, or wild boar. After protracted haggling over price, furniture (it came furnished, but with what, exactly?) and move-in dates, we came to an agreement. Because we were anxious to leave Torralba for our own home, we asked to rent the house for a couple of months in advance of the official sale. The furniture would stay, but the homeowners would haul away their personal effects, such as the large TV in the kitchen and the decorative knick-knacks over the fireplace. A few weeks later, we moved in. Although I had spent Thanksgiving far from my home and without turkey and dressing, I felt like I had a lot to be thankful for. We hadn't been drowning in choices when it came to finding a home, but somehow we had come up with just what we had been looking for. Sometimes not having much choice is a good thing.

The moment the papers were signed, we returned to the house. Our house. Giddy with joy, we ran exultant laps in the lawn's thick grass. *This place is ours.*

In those early months, our heads were filled with visions of our future lives as *contadini*. Neither of us had ever touched a lawnmower or a pair of hedge clippers, but suddenly, we were fixated on cutting lawns and trimming back the garden's long thicket of hedges. I had never raised anything more demanding than a houseplant, and suddenly I was thinking about planting zucchini and bell peppers, pruning back plum trees and trying to figure out how to prevent hungry aphids from sucking the life out of our oleanders. I had mailed over thick gardening manuals from the United States (written, unhelpfully, for a North American climate) and we flipped through them constantly, fantasizing about improvements we could make. We envisioned a new stone wall—elegant, graceful, Old World. A flagstone garden path could provide a functional yet charmingly picturesque passage about the grounds. Umberto imagined a swimming pool. It was all so tantalizingly foreign from how either of us had grown up. Finally, I had the sensation of writing my own life's script rather than sleep-walking through life on the expected path. It was all new to Umberto too, but still, it was his country, his language, and a version of his people, although it is true that Sardinians were generally shorter than mainland Italians and spoke in clipped *Sardu* that sounded the way Italian might if it were spoken backward. He had more familiarity with Italian country ways, as his family had spent every summer in the small mountain village of Caporciano, located in the region of Abruzzo, about an hour and a half east of Rome. (Each time we visited he pointed to a nearby village on a hill and exclaimed proudly, "That's where Madonna's family is from!") He was used to how quiet it could get, how fast the weeds could grow, how nosy the neighbors could be.

We had more space than two people and a big dog knew what to do with, so we mulled over starting a home-based business, maybe a bed and breakfast. Every dissatisfied professional back in the States seemed to be forsaking his or her office cubicle for the quirky life of innkeeper. I tuned in daily via satellite TV to a program on Home and Garden Television called *The Good Life* featuring these burnt-out professionals, some of whom were Americans who had settled in some quaint foreign locale. Why not us? We could grow tomatoes, zucchini, and strawberries. We could make jam from our pear and plum trees. We could eat wild fennel. I had never heard of chicory before. Now visiting friends plucked it from the side of the road and boiled it up for dinner as a rustic green feast. Coming from the urban snarl of places like Rome and L.A., there was nothing more glamorous in our eyes. The technical details of running the house appealed to Umberto, accustomed to thinking of systems and circuits and designs. And I, myself, had nurtured a passion for house and home since my childhood days spent touring model homes on L.A.'s eastern edge with my parents. I had always enjoyed looking at houses, thinking about redecorating them, living in them, visiting open houses, which must have somehow led me to one of my most "natural" jobs as a journalist—editor of the At Home section of *The Boston Globe*. As a reporter, I had written features on the changing image of the "bachelor pad," how young couples scrimped and saved for a down payment on a house, how older couples divided up the housework, and the fairness or unfairness of it all. As an editor, I commissioned articles on inventive uses of space at home, as well as profiles of notable architects and furniture designers. It was an easy fit for someone interested in aesthetics, design and the minutiae of life at home. And now, finally, I got a chance to try my own hand at the housing game. For me, the house in Sardinia was a sort of stage set for my redesigned life. Plus, Sardinia itself represented a challenge. Would we be able to hack it here?

All the excitement over the house and garden lent our lives purpose and an odd sense of freedom. I knew I was in over my head when it came to all the technical workings of the house, but I didn't let myself think about that too much. On Sundays, we would pull out the cheap bikes we had bought in a bike store in Alghero, and bike to the newsstand at the airport, about ten kilometers north of the city. There, we picked up copies of *Art & Decoration*, a French interior design magazine I had taken a fancy to. On our way, we would pass our neighbor at the end of the lane we lived on. He, at 90 years old, was on his bike too, as he was every day, on his way to his *campagna*. In fact, he biked right past us.

One Sunday afternoon after a bike ride followed by a leisurely lunch, I sat absorbed with *Art & Decoration* as Umberto sprawled out on the rather uncomfortable couch that came with the house. He was watching the incessant buzzing of Formula 1 on TV as the announcer repeated the magic mantra "Schumacher... (fast Italian) ... Schumacher, Schumacher!"

I interrupted all that.

"What if we decorate every guest room differently?" I posited. "We could build "cabanas" out in the lawn, each decorated according to a theme! We could have an African room and a Mexican room!"

Umberto was always open to something new. It was a trait he had picked up from his busy, agreeable mother, who despite her strict Catholic upbringing, embraced novelty, or at least tried to understand it. He was very different from his older brother who quickly snuffed out most of his wife's schemes with a snort of disapproval. Franco, Umberto's older brother, was a softer, gentler version of Umberto's silent, intractable father. Umberto, on the other hand, was never silent and fortunately, very agreeable—especially to this idea. Or perhaps he had been lulled into pacification by the buzzing race cars.

On most Saturdays, we enthusiastically scissored through the wide swath of green grass behind the handles of a gas-powered push mower, a sweaty two-hour job, and I spent long hours on weekday afternoons while Umberto was at work on my knees wrestling weeds out of flower beds. I became obsessed. I had been told time and time again by my parents how impatient I was. I liked to act quickly and brashly to cut to the chase and simplify complicated things. Maybe I was doing a little bit of that now, working ceaselessly to whip the property into a state of perfection it was never meant to have.

"Are you still out here?" asked Umberto's younger brother, Marco, while visiting. The sun had slipped below the horizon, and the mosquitoes were beginning to gather in a cloud of delight around my arms. I was barely visible behind a bed of rose bushes that seemed determined never to flower. I, on the other hand, was determined to force blooms from these recalcitrant spiny shrubs if it took the very last ounce of my strength. I thought back to my father doing yard work on Saturday afternoons in L.A. Back then, it had all seemed so neat and contained. Now maintaining a house and yard felt like a massive whale of a job that was swallowing us alive. In the evenings, Umberto, created drawings on how we might reconfigure the house that looked a lot like the intricate engineering diagrams he drew up for his research projects. He spent hours and hours hunched over the computer, designing and redesigning without benefit of fancy computer software. It was all lots and lots of work, but somehow in all the pain of it, it was also fun. Even though we were doing nothing special in the garden, and much less than our neighbors surrounding us, I felt myself to be a beatnik in my oversized denim overalls smeared with dirt. I was an iconoclast who had escaped a conventional American life of chain stores, strip malls and timed traffic lights to immerse myself in a completely different reality of the *motozappa*, September grape harvests and festivals commemorating cherries and sea urchins and fava beans. It was a rhythm of life that, while slow, also felt infinitely more interconnected and earthbound than the glib, depthless fashion shows I had covered for work.

I also felt free of the boxes that had so much defined my American life. In the United States, I had fought a strange feeling as a child. I sometimes felt less of a person than a category to which a series of preferences and predilections were assigned. I was black, so I wasn't supposed to spend hours practicing Beethoven's Fur Elise, as I did. I wasn't expected to pass hours sprawled on the floor of the family den, nose in a book, immersed in tragic tales told by the likes of Charlotte Bronte, Jane Austen or Edith Wharton. In fact, in third grade at the age of 8, my grade school teacher, Ms. Zepps, had instead foisted upon me *The Autobiography of Malcolm X*, which I consumed as voraciously as I did all the other books that came my way. In my neighborhood, reading and writing and playing classical music meant that I was "acting white." I was the dreaded "oreo"—black on the outside, as white as creamy sugar filling on the inside—and I would forever be condemned to that status.

I never felt completely free to pursue the interests and diversions that naturally interested me. Society had already chosen for me the outlines and boundaries of my life, and I just didn't get it. As far as I was concerned, the skin I was in, my class and station in life, was just a random spin of the wheel. I could just as easily have been born in Ireland or China or India or Indonesia. I could have grown up male, or Muslim or a eunuch in someplace where being a eunuch is a thing. Knowing that my status on the earth was just a twist of fate, a roll of the die, I could do nothing other than identify with who I was beyond this lifetime's suit of clothes. I was simply human. And plenty of times, if not most of the time, I didn't even feel that. I identified most strongly with the dogs I kept as companions since childhood. Once, when one of my aunts made a comment about a dog being "just a dog" I remember as a child feeling like that wasn't the truth of the matter at all. Dogs are so much more than humans. Couldn't she see that?

But in Sardinia, I had stepped outside those prescribed bounds that are so much a feature of American life into something completely different. No one knew what to make of me. The box I was supposed to check and then dwell in for the rest of my life, was a lot fuzzier than in the

United States. I didn't have to pick a tribe because, clearly, I was just me, my own singular oddity.

On weekly phone calls with my parents who were in the process of moving from Los Angeles to Las Vegas, I described what the place looked like and what we had done.

"When can we come to visit?" asked my parents each time. Despite the magnitude of the move I had made, they were supportive. Like many Americans, my parents liked forward movement.

So, what were we looking for? Adventure? Reinvention? Or perhaps it was simply the challenge of immersing ourselves in someone else's life entirely, the way I used to do as a kid reading James Baldwin and Thomas Wolfe novels, and before that, Nancy Drew and Phyllis Whitney. For sure, we were building a new identity as a couple, and the building of a home had everything to do with that identity. When we lived together in Boston, Umberto had joined me in my world, embracing the American rituals I had cultivated like Sunday morning brunch with bagels, surrounded by friends and stacks of newspapers. For a brief few weeks, living together in Rome at Umberto's parents' house, we embraced his Italian rituals of elaborate meals at home with his parents, stuffing down great quantities of his mother's famous mushroom risotto, her *"frittata tonnata"* (a crepe-like dish of eggs with tuna) and her *pasta e fagioli*, a tasty peasant dish of short pasta with Italian beans. When we weren't overeating at home, we overate in pizzerias, choking down pizza of *salmone e panna,* (salmon and cream) with Umberto's high school friends.

But now, on this foreign island in this strange land, a place new to both of us, we were forging a whole new identity as a couple that was built neither on the foundations of Umberto's old life in Rome nor on the remnants of my old life in Boston. We could get to know each other while learning how to appreciate Sardinian specialties that were new to both of us, like sea urchin spaghetti, cuttlefish ink ravioli, and of course *seadas* (a fried cheese pastry doused with lemon and honey.) In a sense, I was getting to know Umberto for the very first time, more on his terms, in his country. Plus, this was our very first house. Sardinia had become a canvas for our dreams.

Our first renovation projects were simple attempts to make a mark on a house that had been completely furnished to someone else's taste—someone who was much older, more conservative and much more serious than we were. Since we were young, we wanted a house that felt young—warm, playful, a bit ethnic in flavor, filled with pattern and color. We didn't want to do the usual. That was boring. We had brought over several pieces of wooden furniture carved in Mexico, bought when we knew we were moving to Sardinia, but before we actually arrived. Somehow, the carved sunflowers on a rough-hewn armoire spoke romantically to our new rustic lives and even recalled some of the finer carved furniture that was part of Sardinian tradition. We hadn't anticipated finding a completely furnished house from the outset. And so, as it turned out, we had more furniture than we could stuff into our very few modest-sized rooms. The armoire sat encased in plastic on our veranda until we could find a place for it. Still, we wanted to keep our Mexican furniture. It was the first furniture we chose together as a couple.

Inside the house, the very first thing we did was paint. One day, while Umberto was at work, I decided I would rub down our plain white walls with a paint called *rosa*, a glowing pink, which I hoped would warm up the house, at least visually. I was up on a ladder in my striped overalls, applying paint with a rag in a large swirl pattern like I had seen in Sardinian restaurants. It would be the perfect backdrop to our Mexican armoire with its cheery carved flowers.

"It's beautiful!" Umberto, always the optimist, declared when he saw it.

We had new slipcovers sewn using a fabric that recalled a Mexican blanket. We hung our own pictures, some of which I had painted as "outsider" art, without knowing I *was* an outsider. And we played around a lot with furniture, dragging it from room to room, trying it for a while in the living room, then putting it into the bedroom. What had been a small bedroom with a bunk bed became a study with a single guest bed. The house began to feel a little less stiff, a little more "us." The décor was neither sophisticated nor chic. It had a naif quality, thanks to our age and our lack of money. Still, it was ours, something very different from what you would find in either Rome, Boston or L.A. And it was something we did together.

We lived through our first winter in which it quickly became evident that the thin, rattling windows were completely inadequate to their task. Wind whistled, with purpose, right through the panes. I was so cold I spent most of my time swaddled in a wool blanket like a preemie infant in an incubator, a portable gas heater at my feet. The central heat, powered by propane fuel, was no match even for the relatively mild Sardinian cold. My fingers turned blue with the chill, and my feet, even in wool socks, felt like ice cubes. I began to recall, wistfully, my old overheated apartment in Boston. The darkness of the place, particularly on short, overcast, humid winter days started to eat at us too. Even on bright days, we relied on artificial lighting just to go about normal tasks. To escape the inky dampness of the house, prone to humidity and mold in the winter, I took to spending my days out in the garden, warming under the sun like one of the geckos that scurried across our walls. My permafrost feet defrosted for a while. There were some afternoons when I had no choice but to flee outside. Electricity was never a sure thing, and quite often, we found ourselves without power, which aside from meaning we had no light, also meant we had no heat and no water (our water came from a well run by an electric pump). There were many days in the house when I felt like I was living in more of a *campeggio*.

But aside from all this, the humidity, the dimness, the thin, jangling windows and even the occasional rat scampering overhead across the veranda rafters in the evenings, (we named him Eduardo, after no one in particular), the one pressing desire we had beyond all others was for more living space. To be specific, we needed a guest room. We had a tiny little house, no more than about 800 square feet. The fact that we had a little bit more than one acre of garden did not compensate for the space deficit, it only enhanced the campground effect.

When friends with children came to visit in those early years, we were awakened at dawn by screams and cries that echoed throughout the house, loud, as if they were coming from the very next room. (Because they were.) Elena and Simone, who were some of our first visitors, tried desperately to quiet the cries of their little toddler Matteo, who flailed about the house in high spirits each morning. But the house did not forgive. Our bedroom opened directly on the kitchen, like one of those shotgun shacks in the American South, and the kitchen was the only communal space. When the morning light was still faint, just barely crawling through the window of the front door, I heard loud whispers. "Matteo, no! Matteo, *zitto!*" And so, the day began.

Because our idea of opening a bed and breakfast was beginning to seem more real (it was the only professional option for me as a foreigner in Sardinia if I didn't plan on teaching English) it was clear the most viable plan was to follow through on the idea of separate guest bungalows built around our huge lawn. This project began to take precedence in our minds as the pace of visitors picked up with each passing summer so that we rarely spent a summer week alone.

The most obvious place to build the first guest house was the carport.

Because of strict Sardinian laws regulating the square footage of any structure in what is deigned an "agricultural" district, we could not build any new permanent structures on our land. Most Sardinians in the neighborhood flouted this law by cleverly burrowing underground. The result was huts that looked Lilliputian above ground, featuring basements the size of an airplane hangar down below. In these cavernous spaces, Sardinians built second kitchens, extra bedrooms, a bathroom or two, and certainly a great room to accommodate populous family dinners and extravagant Sunday afternoon gatherings. Our neighbor Pietro set up his psychotherapy office in his commodious space down below. We, however, didn't have that option. Our house, originally just a toolshed, had already been built. It included a very small "cantina" just large enough to hold a couple of barrels of wine. Bulldozing the house to dig a giant hole was out of the question. The only other existing structure on our property was the carport which stood on the other side of the driveway, perpendicular to the house. If we could convert that into a guest house, mindful that at some point (*wink, wink*) it would have to be converted back into a garage as per Italian building codes, then perhaps we had a solution.

And the potential of the carport was clear. It stood across from the house on the other side of the dirt drive lined with oleander trees. It was, therefore, close enough to the main house to be convenient but still set far enough away to be private. It was perfect in dimensions—about the size of a large motel suite that could comfortably accommodate two queen size beds. There was even a little *armadio attrezzatura,* that had been relegated for potting mix, motor oil, and the lawn mower, that could easily become a bathroom with enough space for a toilet, bidet, vanity and a generous shower stall.

We set about finding a contractor who might do the work. After talking with neighbors, it was quickly apparent that there was one man to handle the job. Literally. Although undoubtedly there had to be other *muratori* (or contractors) working in the neighborhood, Soldano turned out to be the *muratore* who had built just about every house in the area, cement block by cement block. If there were other *muratori* around, we didn't hear about them.

Soldano was a short, talkative man who had the air of a swashbuckler about him. The world seemed a stage for his theatrics. Eternally curious, he loved to gossip. He couldn't be too old, considering the hard, manual labor he did, yet he had a ruddy roughened face that suggested a man of about 60. He was probably actually in his early 40s. He wore a knit cap and often a fisherman's sweater which seemed to fit his rough, outdoorsy swagger. Being a buccaneer sort with a pirate's air, he beguiled us with stories of his strength and fortitude. He told us how he had yanked out his own tooth after tiring of a persistent toothache. He finished his story by opening his mouth wide to show the proof. And yes, there was a big jagged hole where several of his teeth should have been. Over the next few years, as we pursued one renovation project after another—a new septic tank, a new platform that might serve as a base for a second guest house, an attic conversion and some major structural work in the main house—Soldano, and his small, loyal crew of workers, became a fixture. From him, we learned how some neighbors got into awful fights that even included violence, and how others had been broken into when they had left the house for long periods of time. We heard stories about his wife's health and his workers' troubles. He asked a lot of questions, undoubtedly to transmit whatever pollen grains of news he could gather from us to leave with his next clients, a bee buzzing from one *corbezzolo* flower to the next.

"You want to turn this into a guest house?" he asked in Italian, surveying doubtfully our little carport—essentially just two walls set against a concrete fence surrounding our land. "*Ma abusivo?*"

No, we explained. It would be legal. It would be a structure that could not be considered permanent, as we were essentially doing nothing more than adding a wall of glass windows to create a room. If we ever wanted to, all we needed to do was bust open a few windows to turn the whole thing back into a very nice garage complete with a wood-paneled ceiling, a ceiling fan, and a nice bathroom.

After a few weeks of hearing gossip from Soldano, along with the perpetual hum of the cement mixer out in the driveway, the guest house began to take shape. It featured textured white walls, undulating, and organic. We installed three simple stone wall sconces. We chose rough, unpolished ceramic floor tiles in a neutral pink, (pink is neutral in Sardinia). We stained the wooden beamed ceiling a lustrous reddish mahogany, making the room feel softly welcoming. The best feature was an entire wall of floor-to-ceiling windows planed and finished by a local *falegname* or carpenter. In the bathroom, we chose an inexpensive dark wood vanity with a country look from the Brico Center, the Italian version of Home Depot, and simple white shower tiles that were ever so slightly *ruvido*. The effect was warm and unpretentious, comfortable and homey. Everything was simple because we had no money. We brought in the few pieces of furniture we had shipped over—an iron bed, the Mexican armoire that we could finally move off the veranda, an extra single bed that had been part of the furniture that came with the house, and a carved Mexican screen and mirror. They were the perfect simple but colorful touches. If every room were to have a theme, this could be our Mexican room. Later we added a vivid green, and red rug loomed and knotted in Nule, a Sardinian village known for its rugs, which had a South of the Border feel about it. The old carport had been transformed into a charming guest room, perfect for a bed and breakfast. We were so pleased with the effect, youthful, open and congenial, that we took to sleeping there most nights, as it was far drier than the humid main house, where mold grew as fast and thick as moss in our clothes, shoes, and books during the wettest winter months. We invited our friends Simone and Annarita, he from Tuscany, she from Naples, to view the finished product. They were unabashed in their honesty: *il box è diventato la piú bella stanza della vostra casa*. The garage has become the nicest part of your home. The only remaining problem was the rest of it.

Giuliana, a friend of ours who worked at Umberto's university, had finally purchased her "forever" home. After living in an apartment in Alghero with her two sons following an acrimonious divorce, she had decided she wanted more space—a house in the countryside. Following many months of sifting through house listings, she and her new companion, Virgilio, found a very rough gem—an unfinished house of concrete block and dangling electrical tubes, set among rolling hills overlooking olive orchards, vineyards and palm trees just south of town.

Umberto and I, always on the lookout for ideas we could steal, paid Giuliana a visit.

"*Eccola*!" said Giuliana, one Sunday that we stopped by. It was before work had truly started, so there was a lot that depended on our own imaginations. We could see the potential—it had much more, in fact, than our own house had. The footprint of the house was larger, and the surrounding countryside more scenic. The shell of the house was surrounded by olive and fruit trees and several grand old palms.

"This room is going to become the living room, and this is where the kitchen will be," Giuliana narrated in Italian as she ushered us through the house. "Up here we're going to put the master bedroom."

In the following months, there was the usual maelstrom of drama and disgust that surrounds every major renovation—that is, disagreements with the architect about the direction of design, delays in when the house would be delivered, mix-ups and misunderstandings about what materials would be used. And Giuliana wasn't the only one going through architectural turmoil. By now, several of our friends had decided to live in the countryside surrounding Alghero. It had become fashionable. Each of these friends had stories to tell of unyielding, rampaging architects. We met from time to time to swap tales. Sometimes, Giuliana joined us. One friend of ours with the most dramatic story ended a long friendship with an architect she had hired to renovate her apartment. The friend, it seemed, was making unapproved changes, and would take offense when questioned about them. Finally, about two years after the initial work began, Giuliana moved into her new country home and invited us over for a celebratory dinner.

When we pulled through the front gate, everything from the outside appeared pretty much the same. There was still disorder in the yard, where an old table once served as a staging space for pizza parties during construction. There was an overturned bucket, used as a stool, and some old tottering chairs near the driveway. But when we got past all that and walked through the front door, we were stupefied. We had entered some sort of high-gloss movie set.

"Wow!" we said, our mouths open.

Every detail shone brightly with love and attention. The starkly modern kitchen cabinets and polished concrete floor looked like something out of *Art &Decoration*. Giuliana had a beautiful, metal staircase custom built. Each step was honed of polished walnut. Ethnic art, textiles, and curios from her travels around the world gave the space a sophisticated, eclectic vitality and warmth. Light flooded through oversized sliding glass doors that opened to a patio overlooking Mediterranean rolling hills. Although the décor was essential, it was not minimal. No expense had been spared, but you could see that Giuliana had not emptied her wallet on "easy" status items designed to impress others, like trendy and expensive commercial ovens or designer couches. Rather, she had turned her attention to the details—the wood she used on the staircase (not easily available in Sardinia), the tiles she had brought back from Morocco. She must have spent tens of thousands of Euros to buy and renovate this property. And she was an assistant professor. Assistant professors can survive in Italy, but they are by no means rich. But that's the thing about Italy and Italians. A person needn't be rich to make the pursuit of beauty a priority.

Back home, it had always seemed to me that interior design, art and beauty was the province of only the upper classes. Everyone else, it seems, was just trying to pay for healthcare, an education for their kids, and put some money away for retirement. These are reasonable, practical goals. But in Italy, quite possibly *because* these basic needs are largely taken care of, there was room for what might at first feel superfluous. Even a truck driver of modest means spent time and energy on beautifying his surroundings. And let it be understood that men are just as interested in refinement and style as women. I would always remember one scene I saw at an Oviesse department store in Rome. A middle-aged man was shopping with his wife, who was evidently on the hunt for a new blouse. He selected a silky blue shirt from a sale rack and held it up for inspection.

"Now this would look stunning with that leather skirt of yours," he commented in Italian.

I tried to imagine a similar scene back in the U.S., where men stoically planted themselves on benches outside of stores while their wives picked through the sales racks, alone.

One day, I visited my friend Margherita. She was a friend I made early on in Sardinia, when I decided I would do what all English-speaking foreigners seemed to do if they were in Italy for any length of time—and that's teach English. I was teaching English at the same school I had attended as a student in those first few months in Sardinia. (Upon completion of my first course, the school director, seeing an opportunity to exploit my language skills as a native English speaker, invited me to teach as a freelancer, schooling employees of local businesses and firms in the English they might need to conduct business.) Margherita had been one of my students in an English class I had taught to the employees of Alghero's airport, where she had been a secretary. Over time, we developed a friendship. Every now and then, in the mid-afternoon, I showed up at her downtown Alghero apartment where we chatted and sipped tea during the town's *"pausa"* when most of the stores were closed. We timed the visit strategically, so that we could finish our tea and cookies by about 5 p.m., just as the town's stores began to re-open. That's when we would stroll down Alghero's cobblestoned center to take in a bit of village life. Margherita loved art, design and fashion, and those topics formed the basis of our relationship. We often visited the store of Antonio Marras, who had made a name for himself in Paris for clothing inspired by traditional Sardinian dress. This time, upon entering Margherita's apartment, an apartment I had visited just a few days prior, I could see that everything was different.

"What's happened here?" I asked her. "Everything's been moved!"

A couch that had been under the window was now facing the window. A chair that had been in the corner of the room was now in the middle of the room. Her dining table had moved across the room too. And it all looked fantastic.

But it shouldn't have surprised me. Every time I visited Margherita, the furniture, paintings, rugs, moved. In fact, the furniture moved so often you would think it was alive.

"It's like a hobby for me!" she said by way of justification.

"Do you think I should move this lamp?"

It was not just Margherita. Margherita's beau, likewise, had spent an equal amount of time choosing original art for his dental office, and lovingly tending plants and collecting antiques for his modest *campagna*. One Sunday afternoon that we visited, we marveled about how his little country house felt like something out of a movie set.

I thought a lot about what made Margherita and her boyfriend Antonio so different from those who might have been their equivalents back in the United States. I decided it came down to this: when Italians buy a house, it's for their entire lives. There is very little "house-flipping." So consequently, people like Margherita, or Giuliana, or any of our friends, were unafraid of "wasting" money to make things nice. No matter how much it might cost, no matter how much longer it might take, no matter how much easier or cheaper the ugly choice might be, they always studied their choices with attention and went that extra mile for the beautiful. (Without getting into crazy debt, of course.) Furthermore, it was not just about beauty to be put on "display." They enjoyed private, unseen beauty, too. Italians spent countless hours beautifying the backside of things and underneath. Wall outlets were not an afterthought. They were chosen with the attention you would give an object of honor, like a painting over the fireplace. Once, touring the "chef's kitchen" of an upscale apartment in a "luxury" American condominium building, Umberto scowled at the bright white outlets dotting every few inches of a black granite backsplash. "That's horrible!" he said. "And they think this is elegant!" In another American kitchen we saw, Umberto registered his disbelief that the carpenters had not bothered laying floor tile down all the way to the wall underneath the cabinets. Evidently, they figured no one was going to look back there anyway. At least no *American*.

In one of the many conversations Umberto and I had on this topic, I tried to explain the mysteries of my people.

"Americans are practical," I explained. "We don't trust our own taste, probably because we aren't brought up around all the beautiful palaces and frescoes and sculptures the way you guys are. You guys see all that stuff from the moment you leave your mothers' wombs. It comes naturally for you. And what do we Americans have? Strip malls, big box stores and billboards."

I went on.

"It must be something about our Puritan roots that has us feeling that putting too much importance on how something looks is shallow and superficial."

"Well, in Italy, it's not superficial," Umberto responded. "I mean, *certo*, everything's got to be functional. But form contains function. That's what makes Italian cars and motorbikes the best in the world."

"I know what you mean," I agreed. "Have you ever noticed how chunky and awkward American vacuum cleaners are?"

"Or," added Umberto, "kitchen faucets, or lighting fixtures?"

"And American couches are always beige!" I lamented. "They are big, flabby and shapeless and they've got cushions that look like cows' udders!"

Clearly, I had become a European design snob.

To me, there was truly something spiritual, an acknowledgment of our human desire to connect to something larger than ourselves, in taking time to appreciate something beautiful rather than hurrying through onto the next thing. Spending extra money on beauty diminished the importance of money, because it meant there were higher values in life then just fattening a bank account. And taking the time to *create* something beautiful just for beauty's sake, to embrace the playfulness of it all, well, that was completely transcendent.

That's when I began to understand about the *peperoncino* in the tomato sauce. Umberto's mother had always told me that the secret to her resplendent pasta and risotto dishes was "*aglio, olio e peperoncino.*" Beauty is that extra spice that gives Italy that extra depth and nice umami flavor missing in the bland United States. It's one reason Americans are fascinated by the country. In my first visit to Italy a few years prior, at a time when I had been feeling despondent and spiritless, Italy had wrapped its arms around me to offer solace, like a loving, sympathetic aunt who, in addition to her solicitousness, knew how to dress well. Now I lived in my aunt's splendid home with all the details attended to, and, at least for the time being, I lived happily, following her example.

REVAMP

There are two kinds of house problems. There are the easy kind, light and fluffy, fun even, to flip over and over in your mind, like a spongy pancake on a warm griddle. And then there are the other kind: the problems that make you feel frustrated, anxious and impatient for radical sweeping change. The kind that make you want to fling the griddle to the kitchen floor.

The dark and damp conditions in our Sardinian house were that second kind of problem.

Yes, we loved our house and the sense of vast space outdoors, but after a couple of years in the space and victory in transforming a simple carport into a lovely little guest house, we knew it was time to tackle the unrelenting darkness inside the main house. Even electrically bright sunny days were depressing. It was also cold inside in December, January and February. In fact, it seemed impossible to make the house warm until late June or July. Yes, we could spend the warmer months eating dinner on the veranda and playing Frisbee on the lawn with Tony but inside, we needed light. We needed air. We needed warmth. The Martellis had used the house just during the summer. Perhaps they had never had to suffer through the inky dampness which became untenable in winter. But we lived here year-round.

"We should break through this wall!" I declared to Umberto one day. It had been another day of mulling over how we could improve conditions. The dog was curled at my feet, nose burrowed in his tail. His thick long fur wasn't enough to keep him warm. I was swathed in my usual indoor garb, a thick wool blanket that was a housewarming gift from Umberto's mother. I gestured to the outer wall of our bedroom, the one that abutted the garden.

"Just imagine if we create a big sliding glass door that would go straight out to the garden," I said. "This room could become our living room. We could knock down the wall between the bedroom and kitchen so that the light from the sliding glass door filters all the way through to the kitchen. It would feel big and open, and there would be so much more light than there is now!"

It was as if I had had an epiphany.

"That's a great idea!" Umberto responded, enthusiastically. "We could even build a patio outside the sliding glass doors so we could have another entertaining space. And the patio will help make the house less damp because the water will be deflected away."

"Will that really make a difference?" I asked.

"Are you kidding?" said Umberto. "Come here!" he called.

He opened our front door and beckoned me around a corner to take a look at the lower wall of the house. It was cracking and bubbling from the humidity being absorbed from the ground.

"Right now, every time it rains all that water gets dumped directly into the soil right next to the house," said Umberto, in the same tone he used with his students at the university. "If we extend the platform out just a few meters, it should definitely feel a lot drier in here."

Currently, dry it was not. Flakes of "*intonaco*," the white stucco on our interior walls, drifted down to the floor like snowflakes in a slow-motion blizzard. If we left the room for even just a few minutes, by the time we returned, we would find a new pile of paint chips on the ground.

"The new sliding glass doors are going to be solid, and double-paned," I insisted to Umberto. "They won't be like the awful leaky windows we have now!"

One of my biggest challenges in Sardinia was simply staying warm, which might seem like an odd problem to have on a temperate, Mediterranean island. It's true that I came from a family of heat lovers. Whenever the outdoor temperatures dipped below 65 degrees in L.A., my mother would turn up the heat. As a heat-seeking child, I would stand on top of the grate of a floor heater in our home's hallway for the pleasure of it, like a snake sunning on a rock. It's true, I was a wasteful, comfort-loving American, used to excess instead of thriftier ways. But here in Sardinia, as far as I was concerned, people lived at the other extreme. In the winter time, Sardinians donned coats to go to work and they never took them off. Instead, I saw them huddled in gelid stores and offices wearing parkas all day long, only sometimes ceding to the luxury of a space heater. But I had been too spoiled by the luxury of heat. I couldn't live that way.

Was I simply too stuck in my American mindset, where the primary objective was always comfort and ease? Ironically, it seemed, I had sought out a different culture, only to doggedly attempt to make it more like my own. It was the perpetual trap of travel and expatriation. None of this escaped my notice. However, I still wanted to be warm.

We called Soldano. He arrived with his good-natured crew. If earlier he had thought us odd for putting so much effort into a house that was clearly not meant to be lived in, at some point he had probably realized that our continual house renovations were a reliable and steady source of income for him and his workers. Fortunately, for us, labor costs were probably a quarter of what they might have been in the U.S., which made sense—I had noticed that monthly salaries seemed roughly equal to a very good American paycheck of one week. It might seem small, except taxes and the costs of medical care and education had already been deducted, leaving most Sardinians free of the sort of financial worries plaguing many Americans. So that meant that if we planned carefully, we would be able to afford whatever Soldano proposed.

"Ma questo e' un muro portante!" Soldano bellowed when we showed him the wall in question. In other words, it was not a simple matter of knocking down just any old wall. This particular wall, the wall between the bedroom and kitchen, was a load bearing wall that ran from the back to the front of the house and kept it from caving in on itself. Without it, the house would be just one heap of rubble. On the other hand, the wall between the garden and the bedroom could be knocked down, no problem. And it would definitely bring in a whole lot more light.

But Soldano had a solution to the problem of the load bearing wall.

"Mettiamo un trave," he suggested, sucking on a cigarette. In other words, he was proposing that he and his crew bring in a massive steel beam that would help support the second story and roof of the house. With something like that in place, we could open up the space and get the light and air we craved without compromising the house's structural integrity.

We agreed to his plan. It took some time to get work started, however. First, we had to visit the *geometra,* a type of junior architect used in Sardinia to oversee and approve the renovation and construction of houses. An Italian *geometra* has little training compared to Italian architects, and it clearly showed in the work-a-day banality of most of the houses around us. But that's how things were done. We explained what we wanted to do, and we applied for certification for the work from the city. That took a while to happen.

A few months later, Soldano took a sledgehammer to our interior supporting wall. Rubble and refuse engulfed the house. Finally, the radical, sweeping change we had craved was happening. And it was loud. And dusty. We draped the kitchen cabinets and countertops with plastic and moved the furniture that had been in the kitchen, *salotto* and bedroom out to the veranda, where we draped more plastic to protect it all from the hot gritty winds of the *Scirocco* expected to blow in from North Africa later in the afternoon. We moved ourselves out to the guest house where we could maintain some semblance of sanity amidst all the banging and dust. I brought my computer so I could continue to work and write. I had taken on a few odd jobs doing translation work—an online science magazine called *Galileo*, a gig translating pamphlets for a boat company and, of all things, a job writing a technical manual for a gun manufacturer. I didn't want to miss out on the little work I had managed to cobble together. We used a small refrigerator that we bought for guests, storing our breakfast yogurt inside. Mostly, it was up to me to live each day amid the ruckus. Umberto merrily departed each morning for his job, riding an old bike to the closest train depot—a little house lived in by a caretaker who spent his days tending to the depot's fish pond and strumming his guitar. The chaos of renovation was a convenient excuse to eat out every night, usually pizza. We ate out so often that we named a kitten we adopted *Mattonella* (little tile) after the name of one of our favorite pizzas from a restaurant on the edge of nearby Alghero. It seemed to make sense, considering we were now surrounded by little tiles, bricks and concrete.

It was a change we had craved in the house, but on a larger level, it was a change we had engineered in every aspect of our lives. Renovating and reconstructing the house was a process of reconstructing and renovating ourselves. It was a change I had sought in my life after the shock of my first husband's death. Unlike my first husband, a man of words who wrote poetry and admired the soaring rhetoric of John F. Kennedy and his speechwriter Ted Sorensen, Umberto was a man of action. He believed in building and constructing on a more practical level. He saw me and the world in ways divergent from the way an American would. He didn't know who Ted Sorensen was, but he knew European art and culture and science. He knew what it was like to live in a country that was not considered the leader of the free world. He knew how to handle gypsy children who pestered passers-by in the train station. He knew how to rewire our electrical system. It was a whole new perspective that instantly belied so much of what I had been taught and what I had assumed to be true. Umberto was different, but he was also familiar. He was a fixer and a doer. I liked that.

But Umberto, too, had taken his chances. He had been the smart-aleck kid in school, with thick glasses and an irritating correct answer for every question. (In elementary school, he could proudly recite all the capitals of Europe. By high school, he knew all the capitals of the world.) But he had sought to leave the comfort of his know-it-all roots and his family's cozy nest to build his own refuge. There was something very daring about it. Few of his childhood friends, now school teachers, architects, bankers, graphic designers and functionaries in the Italian version of the

IRS, had ventured outside Rome, much less outside the neighborhoods they had grown up in. Certainly, his parents with their stable government and corporate jobs, did not necessarily encourage him to take crazy risks. Somehow, the very real, concrete transformation of ceiling beams, window frames and floor tiles mirrored a similarly laborious internal adjustment in life goals, cultural norms, expectations.

By now, we had been involved in this house project for about three years. Day by day, we were learning more about the island. We had moved beyond the starry-eyed storybook picture of Sardinia to the true blood and guts of the place. Sardinia, we were realizing, was limited in ways I had not fully appreciated.

Of course, we had ended up in Sardinia not so much because we had chosen the island, but because the island had chosen us. The reality was that when it came to employment, life was more competitive than it ever had been, and especially in certain professions, like academia. An academic had to accept a job wherever it appeared, even if it appeared on the other side of the country. We had seen this time and time again, both in Italy and the U.S. In Italy, we knew of many couples, including Umberto's mentor and colleague in Sardinia, who lived in some far-flung locale, requiring commuting cross-country to a job on the island. Umbertos's colleague lived in Rome with his wife and children part of the week and the other part of the week he spent in a small studio apartment he had bought a few blocks from the university. This was also true in the United States. We knew one couple—a professor of Italian literature and an economics professor—who had lived separately in two different cities in two different states for most of their marriage. Maybe that's what made it work. Gone were the days when one might expect to get a good job in the city one already lived in, buy a home there, raise kids.

But luckily, we both had thrown in our lot to live together in Sardinia. Unluckily, the island was not the easiest place to work.

Teaching English had not been working out. The language school I worked for offered only sporadic assignments, and I regularly found myself frustrated by paychecks that never seemed to arrive. In Sardinia, you could work a job, but you might never get paid. And other things were prone to happen too.

After months of searching for a lead on jobs, Umberto learned that there was a position open teaching English at the university. He prodded me to apply.

"It pays really well," he said. "If you don't like it, you can always quit."

So, in hesitant Italian, I set up an appointment with Signora Vacca, who was overseeing the selection process.

"We will meet precisely at 1:30 p.m. in my office," she told me over the phone. "Don't be late. *Mi raccomando*!" she added menacingly. She gave me the address of the building and directions explaining how to get there.

The morning of the big interview, I was nervous. Maybe this was my big break. I put on my best "teacher's" garb, (a dress rather than my standard jeans) and pulled back my dreadlocks into a very professional chignon. I pulled out a pair of pumps I hadn't worn since the wedding of Umberto's brother. I transformed myself into *Pamela*, the proficient, and efficient English Teacher. After a 40-minute drive and fifteen minutes spent wandering the halls of the university, I arrived at Signora Vacca's door.

It was shut as tight as one of the clamshells littering one of Alghero's beaches. The hallway was empty. It was the lunch hour, and no one would walk these halls until well after 4 p.m.

I waited for about half an hour, but Signora Vacca never arrived. Angry, I left. Now I understood. I was different from Sardinians. I always would be. I took my obligations seriously. I expected to work. Here, work was incidental, an annoying fact of life, that hovered at the very distant periphery of most people's existence. In fact, this was probably what accounted for the Sardinian's famed longevity, I huffed to myself. (Sardinia has one of the highest percentage of centenarians on earth.) No one was so crazy as to let work get in the way of a good life. But for better or worse, I had grown up in a culture in which work was the centerpiece, as misplaced as that emphasis might be. It defined who I was and what I thought about myself. It gave my life meaning. I couldn't seem to shed my cultural training. And I *would* show up at appointments at the right time, on the right day. And I *would* be there even 5 minutes early, damn it! Yes, I could enjoy the sunset, good friends and a great pizza, but I couldn't, like some Sardinian friends, build my existence around these things while ducking my responsibilities and appointments. So I would work, and I would do it the right way. Of course, I still didn't have a job. Signora Vacca never called to explain her absence that day, and I didn't bother calling her to follow up. It felt, as the Italians would say, *inutile*.

And so, the house assumed even more significance as it filled a gap. It was something to focus on in lieu of career, and it seemed to hold the key to the future. If I couldn't find efficiency and no-excuses reliability beyond our gates, at least I could try to concoct some version within them.

As the reshaping of the house continued, we ultimately replaced those thin rattling windows with heavy dark green aluminum windows which slid silently and authoritatively to a close. Snap. Once the interior wall came down and with the exterior wall opened up to the world, we could take in the glorious garden, palm trees, oleanders and what Italian friends called our immense *parco* where we could glimpse rabbits, hedgehogs and the occasional errant turtle from the comfort of our couch. We could also watch Tony nip and bark at the jets of water that shot out from our lawn sprinklers when they came on. It was still damp inside, but a little less damp. The new space was so open and had so much more light that it felt more like a real house and less like a shed converted into a vacation home.

Planning and orchestrating this project, turning over possibilities in our minds, like pancakes—*what if we added blueberries?*—had been all-consuming and engaging. Here we were, in a land where people took the long view, content to wait and wait and wait until the moment seemed right. This, we had to do too, although it didn't come naturally to me. But I now understood how waiting could help prevent mistakes because what might seem like a good idea in one moment, can seem like a quite a bad idea a few months or years later. Hopefully, our decision to live in Sardinia wouldn't one day turn out that way.

Our house continued to morph and transmute, mirroring changes in the area, the island and ourselves. Within the space of just a few years, our region, once considered impossibly far from town by Sardinians, had transformed into almost just another city neighborhood. More people had migrated to the countryside to live full time, some Sardinian, some expatriates. Our neighbors included an English couple, a German family, Sardinians born and raised in Alghero and Italians from mainland cities including Rome, Pisa, and Naples. As the countryside absorbed more full-time residents, the streets eventually got paved. I once relied on the rutted roads to keep speeding cars from plowing into me as I jogged along neighborhood backstreets. That no longer worked. One day, on a run, a car passed so close to me, its tires nearly nicked my Nikes.

"*Vaffanculo!*" I yelled as the car disappeared down the road. What was wrong with these people? On city streets, they couldn't seem to stop staring at me; now, for some reason, I was invisible! I waved my arms and pumped my fists, Italian-style. At least there was no cloud of dust choking my lungs.

The town finally gave us mailboxes and house numbers. (Before that, we'd had neither, and had relied on a post office box in the nearby town of Olmedo. Occasionally, the office would call us excitedly with news, "Signori, a letter has arrived from America. Let's hope it's money!") The old Petticoat Junction-style train depot where Umberto had reveled in leaving his bike each morning leaning against a palm tree, (absolutely unthinkable in Rome), closed. The caretaker was fired, the fish pond dried up, and one day, when Umberto stepped off the train, he discovered his bike had been stolen. We noticed more painted villas and fancier metal gates. The newcomers apparently had the time, money, and desire for flourishes that an earlier generation eschewed.

Umberto was promoted from researcher to assistant professor. He was building up a thriving research lab which attracted talented students from across Italy and beyond. I, on the other hand, was floating unmoored. I had pretty much given up on teaching. It was too infrequent and too badly paid to be satisfying. It had never been my life's dream. We still hoped to run a bed and breakfast. We had even given it a name—"*Casa Nostra*"—if you get the humor. We had managed to rent out our one guest house occasionally, but we also had begun to see that even if we did succeed in building several guest houses (a near impossibility with zoning restrictions), it could never come close to a steady income. The tourist season in Sardinia was concentrated like tomato paste into the small, slim tube of August. (This later expanded into May, June, and July as Italians began to modify their traditional custom of vacationing only in the month of *Ferragosto*). But that amounted to, at most, four months of the year. Maybe five if you counted the cerebral tourists who listened to jazz and sun on uncrowded beaches in the shorter, cooler days of September, after the flashier throngs, women with leathery tans and men in gold chains and tiny speedos, disappeared back into the *periferia* of Rome or Milan. What was I to do with the other seven months of each year? Casting about, I added a very limited amount of freelance writing to my few translation jobs. On the heels of a very robust career, I found my narrow options increasingly frustrating. I was used to deadlines and meetings and colleagues and talking with the public. I was used to having an impact. Now, I had none of those things. My efforts didn't even have much of an impact on our own weedy flower beds, much less anything beyond our gate, in a culture and language I didn't understand. Yes, I had wanted to change my life, experience a different reality, see something new. But I hadn't wanted to erase my very existence.

I couldn't help but think back to my days at the newspaper. I had been surrounded by interesting, intelligent, fun people who would always come through in a pinch. In the newsroom, we had all been about the same age, and there was always some drama going on. Personal stories of affairs, alcoholism, births, and miscarriages, new love lost and found, played out alongside the usual workplace concerns of missed deadlines, story errors, and getting scooped by the city's competing newspaper. Now, I didn't have any of that. I thought back to a going-away party my friends and colleagues threw just before I left, featuring prodigious quantities of alcohol and the thumping grooves of Parliament, Cameo and The Ohio Players. The party was held at the large suburban home of a *Globe* colleague known for blowout bashes in which journalists and boozed out Cambridge poets and artists would make such a racket the police would sometimes show up at the door. Now, that life felt far away. Now, everything was... well...very quiet.

I had a few American friends in Italy, but no one else was in a much better situation, fiscally speaking. No one I knew had anything close to a regular job. Most Americans taught English sporadically in one of the language schools that could be found in most cities. The only American I knew with a solid career was Jason, an American friend with a whole lot of guts, who had concocted his own *codice fiscale* number, comparable to an Italian social security number, and commenced work, illegally, as a consultant with an Italian government office in Rome. Nobody knew the difference. But as for the rest of us, we found ourselves in Italy thanks to love, and it was our loved ones, our partners and spouses, that sustained us not only psychologically, but financially, as we struggled to develop a career.

One day, when a rising feeling of defeat finally erupted into a torrent of tears, Umberto turned to me and made a suggestion. He was Mr. Fix It, after all.

"Why don't you go to art school?" he asked. "It's free!"

At first, the suggestion seemed like a silly one. And then, on second thought, it didn't.

Art had long been an interest of mine. Before I met Umberto, I had satisfied my artistic impulses with evening watercolor classes at the local adult education center. I had no great pretensions, it was simply a way to follow a thread that had weaved its way through my life since I was a child. In elementary school, my parents had taken me to weekend drawing classes for gifted students. In high school, an art teacher proposed that I major in art in college. I rejected that idea in favor of an occupation that might hold the promise of regular meals. Back in Brookline, my handiwork, including a naïve portrait of my deceased pug Tao, adorned the walls of my dining room. Around the time that I met Umberto, my artistic urges had mushroomed into something more substantial. Journalism, after so many years, was beginning to feel trite. I had written every possible story in every possible way. Art and design, though, was a whole new world to be explored. And from what I could tell, it was a world that I liked. As an editor, I had worked with many designers in the department across the hall, and I appreciated everything that went into the job. Working with shapes, forms and colors, felt so much more visceral and organic. It was fresh and more immediate than wrangling with cold type and abstract ideas on a page.

Plus, the souls of the designers I knew twinkled and flickered lightly like sparklers in the hands of children on the Fourth of July. The design department at the Globe had a very different energy from that of the newsroom. While there may have been a few divas, they were a laid-back crew. The journalists, on the other hand, were more like the city-sanctioned fireworks being launched over The Charles. Like artillery shells and bottle rockets, their egos burst into full view, loud, flashy and even dangerous. In my final year at *The Globe*, I had somehow managed to convince my editors to give me a four-day work-week so I might enroll in design foundation classes at the Art Institute of Boston. One day, after a class dedicated to basic rules of composition and color—a class in which we had painstakingly composed grayscale charts according to color values, an exercise that seemed mostly devoid of any creativity, the professor pulled me aside.

"I really think you should become a painter," she had whispered conspiratorially as if she were sharing a secret. What she could possibly base this advice on given the narrow and very basic nature of our class assignments, I still haven't figured out, except, perhaps, that I had some difficulty keeping my palette of grays neatly inside the lines.

And so, one October morning, I applied to the Accademia di Belle Arti. I was greeted at the school by a stern, rotund man with round red glasses and a bow-tie who turned out to be the school's director. He led me to an empty classroom where a human skeleton dangled from a metal rod that had been set in the center of the room. A pad of paper was placed before me.

"Now draw it," the director told me, before slamming the classroom door shut. The door banged shut with a resounding echo, and even the skeleton seemed to shudder. This was my entrance exam. I spent about an hour laboring over my stick-figure drawing. Femur here. Ulna there. Sternum there. At the end of the hour, the school director reappeared, and I presented him with a sketch of a badly deformed skeletal figure that seemed to suffer from scoliosis.

He took it, examining it gravely.

"You're in," he told me, with a handshake.

I loved art school, and the other students—a good ten or fifteen years younger than me—welcomed me. There was a cast of characters—Pierpaolo, the musician provocateur, Rosella, the free-spirited beatnik hippie, Bruna, the been-there-done-that housewife/artist, the only other student who was my age. Being black and American, I was exotic, and my classmates embraced me as part of their tribe of outcasts. It was the closest I had ever felt thus far in my time in Sardinia, to belonging. My professors were continually insisting that I do huge paintings. After all, I was American, born in the land of huge landscapes, huge sky, and huge people. I became obsessed with painting and art. I steeped myself in Giotto and Giorgio Vasari, and was introduced to more contemporary names like Lucio Fontana, Jannis Kounellis, Carol Rama and Maria Lai. We started visiting museums and shows whenever we traveled to the mainland. The Venice *Biennale* became one of our habitual summer trips. And now I bought art magazines in addition to shelter magazines. I saw a strong connection between interior design and art, and one seemed to move along a continuum into the other.

I felt a sense of peace and connection when I painted. Painting was neither analytical nor logical. For me, it was about feeling, emotion, raw sensation, intuition. Colors and shapes pulsed with energy. It seemed the perfect antidote to a life of analyzing people and events, scrambling to fit messy ideas and actions into a coherent, consumable narrative. That must explain why I was so drawn to abstraction, inspired by the splatters of Joan Mitchell, the drips of Pat Steir and the textured smears of Joan Snyder. I liked the imprecision, the fact that there was no storyline, that you could draw your own conclusions. I also liked that anything I might paint might very well end up hanging on someone's living room wall for years. It was nothing like a newspaper article, tossed into the day's trash after a quick read. In those earliest years, I painted abstractions of American canyons and the human figure twisted into abstract shapes. Later on, I moved into full-blown abstraction, emphasizing basic shapes that alluded to something bigger.

While I spent my mornings and afternoons immersed in anatomical drawing, art history, and painting at the Accademia di Belle Arti, a few big changes were going on at home. We enlarged what had been a tiny *pozzo nero* or septic tank, built for vacation use only, to a larger tank that could accommodate the emptying of bladder and bowels on a full-year, permanent basis. We installed a large, outdoor propane tank that we buried underground in our driveway, and we finally graveled the dirt drive that turned to mud whenever it rained. Things started to look a little more polished. When we weren't working on the house, we spent our time doing Sardinian things—hikes up to *Monte Doglia*, dinners at the local *agriturismo*, where a cute baby pig in the afternoon became a savory entrée by the evening. There were days at the beach, trips to the local hot springs, and regular pizza dinners at Pizza Al Metro, our favorite pizza restaurant which served thin, delectable pizzas in flavors like *cinque funghi* (five mushrooms) or *campagnola* (gorgonzola and bacon) by the meter. Our friendships consolidated with time. We began to see more of a tight-knit group, mostly a collection of Italian expats from the mainland, with a few born-and-raised *Algherese* mixed in. We got vegetables from our neighbor Francesco who spent every single day lovingly cultivating his huge, diverse garden of eggplant, lettuce, peppers. One day he arrived at our door carrying a crate of celery, a vegetable I had always avoided. To me, it was tasteless.

"Try this," he insisted. "You must eat it tonight."

He gave me instructions as to how I should prepare it, although because I hate celery, it went in one ear and right out the other. That night, seeing so much celery jammed into the refrigerator, I felt an obligation to try it. I broke off a piece and drizzled a bit of olive oil on top, chomped into a stalk and felt the lights flicker just a bit. It was rich and flavorful and luscious. Here I was, nearing middle age, tasting celery for the first time.

Aside from the smaller house projects, we embarked on two major ones. At the time that we applied to the city to knock down the "*muro portante*," the load-bearing wall which kept the house standing, we also applied to seize errant attic space that was completely inaccessible and thus unused. There was no entry from either inside or outside the house, so it took a little initiative to see exactly what was up there. Umberto discovered exactly what one day when he climbed a ladder to the roof, removed the Spanish terra cotta roof tiles and descended below the roofline. As his head disappeared beneath the tiles, I could hear him exclaim, "There's a lot of space up here!"

"How much?" I asked.

"A lot!" he replied, ecstatic.

From that point on, he made regular pilgrimages inside the roof to ruminate on and ponder exactly what could be done. There was too much potential to be ignored. One day, he convinced me to delicately ascend a perilously shaky ladder to take a look.

"Alright, alright," I said to him, irritated. "I hope this is worth it!"

But after climbing atop the roof and then crawling into the attic space filled with pigeon feathers and bird feces, I could see he was right. We'd had plenty of fights over cock-eyed ideas he had about one thing or another. He was always looking to do something I felt to be fanciful and impractical. For instance, I did not want a pool because I knew it would mean trawling bougainvillea leaves out of the water all day long. (And I knew I would be the one to do it.) But Umberto had a penchant for control, as did I. Being evenly matched in our stubbornness meant we'd had lots of fiery debates about the direction the house should take. But this idea, for a change, held some merit. The dark, unused space ran the full length of our house and was nearly as wide as the house. The sloped roof meant that some of the square footage couldn't be used as living space, but it certainly could be turned into closets. If we could access this space and turn it into a second level of our house, we would nearly double the size of the house, without violating the strict building codes that wouldn't allow us to expand the footprint of the building or to build a new structure. And all that space could add up to another room to rent to summer visitors. I had not been in Italy all that long, but I had learned a lot from Umberto, who, like many Italians, had mastered the art of inventing creative ways to circumvent often perversely inane laws.

We called Soldano. By now he was used to our projects, and always curious to hear our latest scheme. When he came over and he and Umberto clamored up to the roof to peer inside, Soldano, as always, was skeptical. He pointed out that on the low side of the attic, the ceilings were only about four feet high. He pointed out that we were both giants by Sardinian standards—Umberto matches my 5'10 with his 6'2 frame.

"You both are tall," he said. "You'll find it impossible to use this space. *Impossibile!* he added, for emphasis.

"No, it will work," Umberto insisted animatedly. "We can use the part of the attic with the highest ceiling to walk around. The lower parts could be used for sleeping, and the very lowest part of the ceiling toward the edges of the roof as a long, low closet.

Since we already requested authorization from the city for this change when we began to plan to knock down the load-bearing wall, we were ready to go. The official story devised for the city was that we needed to open up new windows on either side of the attic for ventilation. Who could argue with that? For this reason, we said, we also needed to add three new skylights to the roof. (In fact, a window facing the east and a doorway facing west do provide excellent ventilation, especially in hot summer months when breezes on the first floor felt stagnant.) The real reason for the change, of course, was that the little house we had bought was tiny and we simply wanted more space.

Soldano and his crew busted through the cement block on both sides of the house over just a few days, much more quickly than the time it took to renovate the guest house. Again, our home was suffused by dust, but most of it was outside this time. After Soldano did the initial work of opening up the space, we hired a window guy to install forest green aluminum frames in the new openings which would match the new windows downstairs and to punch three more openings in the roof. Our attic now had three skylights and abundant light and air. Next, we hired a floor guy to install a light-colored wood-look laminate, one of the few options we had that would avoid raising the floor level too high. Every centimeter of height was precious. We had an aluminum spiral staircase built which ascended from the patio below to the attic door.

"You won't believe how large it looks!" Umberto marveled to me after the windows were in and the floor was done. "Come and see." He was cute, with his dark tousled hair. These things always made him so happy.

When I saw the space close to complete, I was amazed. Our closed off attic, a mere nest for birds, was indeed large and loft-life. And now, it had a small bathroom in the middle, acting as separation of two spaces that could become two separate bedrooms if we chose. Umberto had been right, despite my protestations. I suddenly felt empowered. Like the canvases I used for painting, the room, with all its light and blank airiness, seemed to offer a multitude of possibilities. The change helped mask the sense of futility I often felt in so many of my daily activities in Sardinia. It's true, no one was ever going to pick up the trash collecting around the *cassonetto della spazzatura* (or dumpster) at the beginning of our street. No one was going to water the dying bushes planted with great fanfare outside the town convention center that year. By the end of the summer, they would be forgotten, dried up and dead in the blasting heat. I was never going to have a big career as an artist, writer, or anything else in Sardinia. That was as clear as the water down at *Le Bombarde* beach. But our attic, on the other hand, was a different story. Our attic looked great.

Itching to get his hands dirty and not just watch other people do the work, Umberto decided he wanted to install the *perlinato*, or the wooden paneled ceiling that would extend across the entire area of the attic, by himself. Secretly, I didn't want him to do this. This was yet another example of Umberto being over-confident of what he could do. Umberto had a bad habit of starting a project with great passion then running out of steam about three-quarters of the way through. He was the same way about everything. He could run fast, but he couldn't stick with a regular exercise schedule. He could cook a wonderful meal when friends visited, but it was up to me to worry about the less glamorous meals that needed to be cooked every evening, without appreciative diners to offer compliments. (And yes, I went jogging every morning, took the dog out for walks each afternoon and cooked serviceable, workaday but relatively healthy meals each evening.) Umberto's fleeting interest in projects and routine was reflected in our house that always felt a little patchworked and incomplete. I wanted a professional to install the ceiling since they usually knew what they were doing, and when they didn't, you could hold them accountable to fix a job badly done. And besides that, this job involved a lot of neck-craning. Anyone installing these panels would have to keep his neck cocked, hammering away for hours, contorted like Michelangelo painting the Sistine Chapel.

"That's the fun part of owning a house," Umberto said. "I can do it. You'll see. Besides, it would cost way too much to hire someone to do the whole ceiling, and I'm not sure who I would ask. *Non preoccuparti!*"

I grumbled to myself. Why couldn't he be satisfied with the basic house and garden maintenance, like mowing the lawn and shellacking the wooden shutters that were cracking and badly bleached out by the sun? Why did those things always fall on me?

And so, this do-it-yourself project began. After Umberto cut insulation to fit each paneled strip, he nailed wood panels tightly into place so they would hopefully not come raining down on our heads. *Rap, rap, rap*! Every night after work. *Rap, rap, rap!* Every Saturday afternoon. *Rap, rap, rap!* Every Sunday morning. I didn't know how many weeks Umberto spent hammering away, only that I got tired of listening to all the hammering. I contributed my own manual labor afterward, on my knees, painting the wood-paneled ceiling in a protective glossy finish.

When the dead attic space was finally transformed into a functional attic loft, I had to admit it looked good. There was a sense of sweeping openness that we just couldn't achieve on the first floor without knocking down a few more walls. We brought up a low bed which we put on wheels, so it could be rolled anywhere within the attic, to keep things flexible. Eventually, we moved a dresser upstairs along with a pull-out couch. We noticed that the upstairs was far drier than downstairs, and with all the skylights and the whitewashed floor with a white oak finish, it was also far brighter. It became my preferred sleeping space in the summer months when refreshing breezes blew pleasantly through to help cool things down. I used the tallest section of the loft, which was on two levels, as a small painting studio, and set up my canvases, paints, and easel. We installed a small sink that was meant to be my painting sink.

After a summer spent sleeping in the attic, we realized we were not sleeping alone. Late in the night, we heard pattering and scuttling above our heads. It sounded like something hairy and large was sliding around above the wood panels that Umberto had spent so much time hammering into place. We grimly surmised that these were either geckos or rats. Geckos we could live with—they were simply part of the Sardinian landscape, viewed almost with affection for their help in controlling the mosquito population. We had no affection for rats, however. This could be a problem.

We realized just how much of a problem after spending some time away in the winter. One month, after returning from a few months abroad, Umberto ventured upstairs to assess how the house had weathered our absence. The windows were sealed. That was good. The *intonaco* had not flaked off the wall. That was good. There were no signs of humidity. Excellent. However, there was something amiss in the long low closet: hundreds of little rat turds speckled the floor. Apparently, a rat with an artistic bent had dined on my collection of paints, creating a bountiful panoply of color and texture as a sort of rat-scale art installation.

"You won't believe what's up there," said Umberto, simultaneously angry and amused.

"Save it all," I joked. "Maybe I can use it on one of my canvases!"

The artist Chris Ofili, after all, was creating paintings from elephant dung and they were selling in the millions.

But this was not the only thing out of sorts in the upstairs attic. It seemed the paneling Umberto had so industriously installed was already starting to sag. A few pieces had tumbled down, like fallen branches from one of our trees out back, exposing the blue Styrofoam insulation material above it. I knew this would happen. It was as sure as the sun rising the next morning. If we (read he) had only accepted the limitations of our (read his) abilities and hired a professional carpenter to install the wood-paneled ceiling, we would never had had to worry about falling panels. And certainly, rats gaining entry would be less of a concern. For the rest of our time in the house, there was always at least one wood panel that dangled from some part of the ceiling. I regarded each dangling panel as a love letter I would have preferred not to get from Umberto.

I wanted to say, "I told you so," but I didn't. When you live with someone, you learn how to hold your tongue.

Initially, it seemed so romantic.

The house came with a vineyard.

"Here it is," Angelo had gestured the first time we had toured the place. He waved his hand before about eighteen rows of pruned vines, bare because the growing season had long passed. "On this side, we've got Vermentino, and on the other side, Cannonau."

I'd never heard of either. My experience of wine was limited to the generic cheap wines served at Chinese restaurants back in the States. In other words, what I knew of wine began with Night Train and ended at Charles Shaw. But here in Italy, we had the opportunity to stretch ourselves and our knowledge of wine beyond Two Buck Chuck. We could do what every self-respecting expat secretly wants to do—create our own wine and then brag about it to our friends.

Even so, the vineyard was still just icing on the cake. Our main preoccupation was not the vineyard but having a place to live and after that a *comfortable* place to live. Getting a little wine out of the deal was a nice little plus, but if the vineyard hadn't existed, we would have bought the house just the same.

Because the vineyard was almost incidental in our minds, it could be said that we did not have a healthy enough respect for the grape. We didn't know varietals and vines, pruning and pests, harvesting and fermentation. But although there was a lot we didn't know, we did know one thing: we needed help. We'd asked Angelo to stay on after we'd bought the house to fulfill this role. Not only would he help us prune the trees and till the land, but he would help us care for the grapevines.

"I guess I could do that," he told us laconically. He said it the way a cowboy might have said it in an American TV drama, except he was speaking Italian.

He stopped by once or twice a week in the beginning to help out. After a few months, though, it became evident, by virtue of his baleful stares and awkward silences, that this arrangement with Angelo wasn't going to last. When he instructed us on what we should do, he often left out critical details that would have made our lives easier. For instance, when our grass caught a disease that spread to all the lawns in the surrounding area, Angelo told us we would need to re-sod the entire lawn, which felt in our minds to be the size of a football field. Instead, it turned out, the grass returned the next season, after the disease had passed. It had just been a sort of grass flu. Angelo, though, had seemed to take a perverse pleasure in scaring us out of our wits. Between the venomous looks he thought we didn't see and his stiff reluctance to be cordial, it was clear that he longed for his old sweet deal with the Martellis who gave him virtual run of the place and ownership of most, if not all, of the wine. Now he had to share both, and secretly or not so secretly, he resented us for it.

"I think we need to find someone else," I said to Umberto one day after more sparks than usual flew from Angelo's side-eye glances. "Angelo always seems to be, well, sort of angry."

"You're right," said Umberto. "He seems to take pleasure in every setback and problem."

In fact, this observation led us to give a name to a phenomenon around the house. When strange and bad things happened at home, we called it "Angelo's Curse."

On the hunt for a solution, we started buying *L'Occasione* again, a habit we had let slip after buying the house. This time, we were focused on the section of ads featuring gardeners.

One ad stood out: *"Sono specializzato in manutenzione giardino, potature di olivo, uva e alberi da frutta, impianto di irrigazione, posa di prato a rotoli. Mi occupo di abbattimento palme di medie dimensioni ed effettuo trattamenti curative."*

Translated, the ad read: *"I specialize in garden maintenance, pruning of olive trees, grape vines and fruit trees, irrigation systems, sodding lawns. I can knock down medium-sized palms and administer curative and preventative treatments."*

In short, this was just what we needed.

When Claudio arrived at our house, we were greeted by a cheerful man of about our age. He was an enthusiastic cultivator, full of passion for pruning trees, which he said was his most favorite activity in the world. He seemed honest, exuberant, hardworking and eternally optimistic—the exact opposite of sullen Angelo. He had loved his job working at a large local *vivaio* which had specialized in growing palm trees, but the nursery had gone bankrupt and all the palms had withered and died. Claudio was looking for another job and although we couldn't offer him full-time work, we could offer a side-gig that could help out a little while satisfying his urge to prune and dig. We had lots of land—many, many hedges, many pine trees and palm trees, a fruit orchard, and of course the vineyard. But neither Umberto nor I was ready to climb our pine trees and prune them back, Italian style. It was perilous stuff. In fact, Claudio wound up in the hospital after falling off a ladder and onto his power saw at another client's home. And this happened to a man who knew what he was doing.

"I can begin immediately," he told us. He showed up the very next day, happily singing in a Sardinian dialect I would never understand.

Thanks to Claudio, the first thing we learned about cultivating grapes was that it was all about timing more than the constant hard work we had imagined. Each winter, before the first green leaves unfurled from the vines, branches needed to be clipped to maximize grape quality. This was when I joined Claudio in the vineyard wearing my striped overalls and rubber boots, reinvented as "Farmer Pam." Claudio belted out songs at the top of his lungs, enjoying the sunshine but ending the peace. He sung out lustily, as if he were in the shower, unashamed about a few off-key wavering notes. After he had done the pruning, together, we painted a thick white coat of lime sulfur on the trunks of each grape vine to protect the wood from rot, a common problem in older vineyards like ours. Sometimes Claudio brought over a borrowed *motozappa* (until we finally broke down and bought one ourselves) to till the chunky clay into soft loam with a lighter, sandier consistency. Each turn of the motozappa blade cleared away the weeds and wild fennel that carpeted the vineyard. In the early Spring, the vineyard needed constant tilling to keep these gluttonous weeds at bay. It was also in the Spring, that the spraying began. Claudio donned a protective get-up which included a plastic jug strapped to his back with a pump spray nozzle. He sprayed sulfur on the vines to help thwart mildew. When the fruit finally appeared, Claudio returned to the vineyard to trim off leaves hanging too close to the fruit. It was essential to clear away these leaves to allow a little sun and air around each grape cluster. Clearing the leaves encouraged the cuticle of the fruit to thicken up. Claudio knew just how many leaves to trim. Too few, and a shaded grape cluster could mildew. Too many, and that grape cluster could burn and shrivel up in the hot sun.

Once the baking, parched summer kicked in, the threat of mildew subsided, and the main concern revolved around sudden pelting rainstorms that could ruin a crop, and hungry birds, which could completely devour it. Sometimes we covered our vines in a net designed to discourage birds. Toward the end of summer, Claudio came by each week to taste grapes for ripeness. If we harvested too soon, we risked a very dry, acidic wine, but if we waited too long, we might end up with a sugary sweet dessert wine. Claudio was the one who called the shots in the vineyard.

In September, when he deemed the time right, we had the *vendemmia*, the crowning event of the season. It involved one day of harvest in which Umberto and I, Claudio and his wife Annalisa, and their children Tommaso and Gina, along with whatever friends we could round up, took to the vineyard to use pruning shears to clip off grape clusters before throwing them into big blue plastic vats which we hauled to our veranda, which had been temporarily transformed into a pressing station. There was always a lot of loud conversation and riotous laughter, because vendemmias, after all, are supposed to be that way. In the September heat, we crushed the grape clusters in a contraption designed especially for that purpose. We turned a crank which controlled an aluminum roller that crushed and destemmed the grapes, ensuring that no grape stems and seeds got into the brew to embitter the wine. The grapes stewed in their own juices for about 48 hours.

The next step involved pulling out the basket press, where grapes are squeezed nearly dry. The juice was then transferred to two large fiberglass vats in our cantina, where it remained to ferment. After fermentation, the juice is poured back into cleaned vats which are sealed with vaseline and left to age until December or January. By that time, it was ready for drinking. There was not much else to worry about except for taking care in the cantina early on, when carbon dioxide build-up could cause you to pass out if you lingered around the vats too long.

We got about 600 liters of wine this way, which we split with Claudio. That gave Umberto and me a few months to polish off 300 liters of wine (we never bothered to bottle our wine but kept it in vats like beer on tap) before the next season rendered another 600 liters. Flying in the face of medical recommendations, we drank wine with dinner each night, and foisted our production on friends and family at every opportunity. We took large jugs to Umberto's father at Christmas; he relished it. We thought for a moment about trying to bottle our homemade production. We also thought about selling some of it to the neighborhood cooperative of growers. We tried a couple of times to take some to the States, where we could share it with our American friends, who were all extremely impressed. But because the wine was organic, without any additives or stabilizers, it didn't travel well. Each time we unscrewed the bottle after a trip, we poured out a pungent vinegar. We regarded the wine the way Sardinians regarded it: as a nice, useful thing to be able to produce out of our land, principally for home use.

Some years, the wine tasted little better than vinegar, even without having traveled. Other years, our wine nearly rivaled that of the professional producers.

What I loved about the wine culture in Italy was the lack of pretense. In the States, wine was an elite pastime. "Decent" wine was supposed to cost at least $20 a bottle, and you felt guilt and shame if your palate was so stunted that you were unable to taste the notes of "chocolate" or "apricot" or "hazelnut." In Italy, wine was a simple, everyday pleasure and people enjoyed it without pressure to taste something that wasn't there. You could get a decent bottle for less than 5 Euros. No one talked about the many things they tasted in wine aside from grapes. That was the approach we adopted. I was quickly learning that when one lives in a culture that fervently believes something and then leaves it to go to a different culture where people fervently believe something else, they experience firsthand true freedom. Suddenly, one realizes that our belief systems hold about as much reality as a child's game of "pretend." You see how beliefs can imprison us, so you drop the beliefs. I was slowly learning to do this when it came to wine and so many other things.

No, we hadn't gone out looking for a house with a vineyard. And no, we never imagined ourselves to be vintners. But now that we owned a vineyard we figured, *"hey, if life provides the grapes, go ahead and make some wine."*

The sun was already bearing down on our heads, but fortunately, we were on our bikes. A salted sea breeze kept us cool as we sped past fields of creeping melon and tomato vines. Every so often, a whorl of gnats formed in the middle of the road and inevitably, one ended up in my eye.

"Hold on a minute," I yelled to Umberto who was ahead of me. "Can you help me get this thing out?"

We biked like this at least one Sunday in every month—either around the countryside or sometimes into town, inevitably ending our ride at whichever *edicola* we thought might carry foreign magazines. We always set out on these rides in the morning, while the breeze was still cool and before the sun became *insopportabile*. Sometimes we biked out towards Valverde, just south of Alghero, where we visited an old church set among dry hills covered in a peach fuzz of golden grass. Other times we biked just north of Alghero, past beaches with emerald waters, and down paved lanes lined with tall eucalyptus trees whose feathery branches brushed the sky. We often finished our ride at the Alghero Airport, where we knew we could find a wide selection of home and interior design magazines. This was one of the things I appreciated about Sardinia. There wasn't much to do here so there was no reason to feel guilty about spending a morning biking in the sunshine, just to buy a few magazines or spending the rest of the day paging through them. This was no guilty pleasure; it was just something to do.

"Oh, look, they've got *Art & Decoration*!" I exclaimed happily while peering into the racks at the airport newsstand. The newsstand was jammed with German, English and French tourists, on the hunt for crossword puzzles or the latest Dan Brown novel. Meanwhile, I grabbed a copy of the French home décor magazine that offered up sumptuous, romantic spreads of artfully inventive interiors, full of color and character.

While I went for my fix of home décor fantasy, Umberto, being the engineer that he was, grabbed a copy of *Maison & Travaux,* or *Casa Facile,* two magazines with a more technical bent detailing the proper steps of all sorts of do-it-yourself home renovation projects, from installing wooden floors to laying down roof tiles. (These were projects I knew he would start and not finish.) We bought several magazines, stacking them in my bike's rattan basket, before eagerly pedaling home, where we ate our Sunday *pranzo* before unwrapping our special treats.

In the way that new parents are totally consumed by the project of having a baby together, we had become totally consumed by the project of having a house together. Of course, newborns and houses are quite different. Houses do not require 3 a.m. feedings (although sometimes we did rouse ourselves at 3 a.m. when we heard the motor of the well groan into action for no discernable reason, meaning that a leak had sprung somewhere.) Pregnant mothers read books like "What to Expect in Your Pregnancy" and then after the birth of the baby, "What to Expect the First Year." We read our shelter magazines.

We'd become obsessed with our project; it had come to represent so many different breakthroughs on so many different levels. It meant forging a life together, breaking free of the lives we had formerly lived, a new way for both of us to indulge our creativity and artistic sides. I had never really had this opportunity with my first husband. When I married the first time, I was just a few years out of college, and we had barely had time to buy furniture before he was gone. Now I was older, and I wanted to create a sense of security, nesting in a new and very different place. In Sardinia, our house had no city water or city sewer system. We lived intimately tied to the earth and a new understanding of how things worked—or didn't. It felt concrete, in a way that the abstract asphalt of Boston and freeways of Los Angeles didn't. In those cities, I was divorced from life's essential activities such as growing food. I had lived, like most city dwellers, disconnected from the fundamental infrastructure of our lives. When I flushed the toilet in Boston, the rush of water swirled around the toilet bowl and that spelled the neat little end to my messy concerns. But oh, nooo, not here. Here, flushing was only the beginning. I knew precisely where my excreta went, and I, alone, had to find a way to deal with it. If, somehow, I let this little problem slide, I could end up poisoning myself and my neighbors. This was the reality of life and confronting this reality was empowering. We were always waiting to see what would come next.

And what came next was always a new project. There was never a time when we felt satisfied enough to settle back in our wicker patio chairs and look around, and think, "it's done." Because it never was. I found the same to be true of painting. Even when you thought you'd finished, if you kept on looking closely, you would find things you'd like to change. Our consumption of shelter magazines, of course, didn't help matters any. It spurred on our never-ending quest for improvement. In the way that eating one potato chip leads to another, our home improvement hunger could not be sated. And of course, fantasy had a lot to do with this insatiable hunger.

In *Art & Decoration*, gravel driveways didn't look like ours. They were not threaded with rabid, vengeful weeds. The countryside was not made up of rural cottages encircled by chain link fences and rusted front gates. The flower beds were not choked with pesky *gramigna, una pianta infestante*. The magazine lawn and patio furniture were always unweathered, or, at most, suggestively weathered, not tottering and frail, like ours. No one tracked mud and dust into these magazine houses. Fallen bougainvillea blossoms did not carpet the patios and bird poop did not encrust verandas. So, there it was, the standard had been flung before us.

We were only talking about pulling weeds, varnishing weathered wood, repairing corroded metal, but it felt like the world was on our shoulders. Would we ever get ahead of all the maintenance? Were we up to it? Would we ever make our home look just a little more like the homes we saw in the magazines? It was a personal challenge.

One of the things I enjoyed about art school was how much it was teaching me not just to look, but to *see*. Sometimes, what we imagine sits right before our very eyes does not sit before us at all. We see our world out of habit, without breaking down the pieces to figure out how they fit together to compose a whole. Now, in my neighborhood and in my own home, as in the art I was studying in school, I was not just looking, but seeing.

Just down the road, Francesco had managed to reach perfection. His land was an impressive vision of pristine order. Precise rows of peppers, cucumbers, celery and zucchini grew unencumbered by weeds. Geraniums spilled out of pots on his veranda. There was not one weathered wooden beam in sight, not one corroded fence, no paint flaking off the corners of his house, like ours. And he didn't even live there! We were envious.

I wondered if my father felt anything like this back in L.A.? He had also fought to make something of our little bungalow that stood so proudly in a neighborhood where some homeowners had just given up, abandoning their houses to decay, weeds, graffiti, and eventually, city action. He had always changed and fixed things, in a restless bid for improvement, of both home and self. My father didn't read shelter magazines, but he had often taken us along to visit open houses on Sunday afternoon, motoring out to distant suburbs where new houses sprung up in the desert like wood-framed cacti. They offered a better vision of a living standard that always seemed slightly out of reach for us in our South Central L.A. bungalow. But oh, did my father try to reach it. Despite the fact that he and my mother were L.A. County employees earning only modest salaries, in the thirteen years I lived in the first house of my childhood, my parents added a darkroom, a fourth bedroom, a third bathroom, enlarged our driveway, and completely remodeled the kitchen. (The last project was after a house fire ripped through one Christmas, leaving behind charred Christmas gifts, walls and floors). Even if some of my father's choices had been questionable—like knocking down a portico which had given the house symmetry to accommodate the family RV—they too had been made optimistically, in a Dale Carnegie-esque sort of way. Both my parents had been restless around the house, always imagining something bigger and better, always desiring more. Perhaps owning bigger and better would make them bigger and better people. Evidently, I had inherited some part of this trait.

"How about if we change the floor tile?" I said to Umberto one day, after leafing through one of the latest editions of *Bravacasa*, my new favorite home design magazine.

We had very dark tile, the color of mahogany or dark cowhide leather. It matched to perfection our very dark wood cabinets. In any other environment but ours, it would have been very elegant. But in our small, dark house, changed as it was with an open concept floor plan and a new larger window to shed more light indoors, it only seemed to make things darker. Plus, the color of the tile varied between rooms. While the living room and kitchen were mahogany-colored, the master bedroom floor was a light pink. The study was a golden blonde. The bathroom was pale gray. The mish-mash of colors and tile patterns looked like a crazy quilt laid out on the floor.

"Yeah, you're right," Umberto agreed. "That will do a lot to make the place feel less dark. But the problem is, if we change the floor, we have to change the kitchen. It doesn't make sense to go to the trouble of lifting all the cabinets to retile the floor underneath, just to put back the old cabinets."

He had a point. The kitchen had always been awkward. The island in the middle of it was so large that no more than one person (usually me) could clean-up and cook at one time. And that one person (also me) had difficulty opening the cabinet doors and reaching down into the deep, dark cavern holding piles of skillets and baking sheets. It was a mess down there.

But in this problem, there also loomed an opportunity. Why not retile the entire house in one uniform tile—light in color, something classic and rustic—and replace the flawed kitchen at the same time with cabinets that were better designed, something where you didn't have to kneel in prayer, every time you needed a frying pan?

If remodeling our house continually was a form of self-improvement, this would be the maximum challenge, offering more redemption and self-development than any adult education course, therapy session or fitness class we could ever take. In remodeling the central guts of the house, we could change the essence of the space. Up until now, we had made tons of changes, but they had always been done at the margins—the carport turned into a guest room, the attic remodeled into a bedroom, a new art studio at the back of our property under a bank of solar panels we'd put up. (One of Umberto's projects.) But this change would alter the heart of the house, the center of the home where we gathered for dinner, entertained friends, watched TV in the evenings.

Choosing the floor was the easy part. We settled on a sandstone porcelain tile that looked like rough stone, and we decided to lay it out in a herringbone *"spina di pesce"* style. More difficult was finding a kitchen. It would have to jibe with the country setting and the rustic flooring, but I still wanted it to feel young and modern, like us and the paintings I created. In painting, I had felt compelled to bring a spare essential quality to the canvas, filled with space and air. And now, it felt natural to extend that feeling beyond the bounds of the canvas. I wanted my dramatic abstract canvases, filled with color and energy, to feel at home. And yet, with all the spare modernity, I didn't want a modern kitchen to feel out-of-place, the way I sometimes felt in Sardinia.

A name surfaced around this time, someone who, even in a small town like Alghero, we had never heard of before. The name was Gianpaolo, the Kitchen God. It turned out that Gianpaolo, in his 40s, attentive, neatly trim with a closely-shaved head, had just redone the kitchen of Tricia and Duncan down the road, two English expats who moved to Sardinia around the time that we had, and they had very good things to say about him. Tricia and Duncan offered the closest point of comparison in all aspects of our lives, not just kitchens. Trisha and I were both readers and regularly exchanged novels written in English. We both had had full careers in our home countries. Trisha had been a nurse and mid-wife in Manchester, England. In Sardinia, we both lived in small houses on big plots of land, in houses that weren't really designed for year-round habitation, so we understood intimately each other's woes. Like me, both Trisha and Duncan taught English before becoming discouraged by the disorganization of the Italian system. They also owned dogs, and we sometimes walked our dogs together out in the woods near Lake Baratz. (It was Tricia's dog Molly, in fact, that ran ahead one afternoon to provoke a wild boar out of its lair. It was as big as a Smart Car and as ugly as any Hollywood movie monster, but fortunately it elected to charge past us, not at us.) Like ours, their house was dark too, but Gianpaolo's kitchen had made their dark home feel bright and efficient. The white Carrera marble top paired with enameled aqua cabinets made everything feel light, cheery and happy. We knew we had to get Gianpaolo.

As soon as we could, we visited Gianpaolo's small store which, after all these years, I had somehow missed on via Don Minzoni, a couple of blocks down from Giardini Martin Luther King. We flipped through several of his fat kitchen catalogs and toured his showroom models of kitchens far beyond our budget. As we examined the models in the store, I got the peculiar sensation of shopping in a jewelry store. Everything felt precious. Everything shone. It was nothing like the tedious traipse down the appliance and cabinetry aisles at Lowe's. We scheduled a time for Gianpaolo to stop by the house, so he could see for himself exactly what he would be working with.

A few days later, he came by.

Why don't you use this wall?" he suggested, gesturing to a wall that was not currently used for anything other than stashing the trash bin. "Let's put in a few open shelves, too. Otherwise it can get pretty heavy looking with so many cabinets." He took scrupulous measurements and promised he would have a sketch for us soon.

The excitement of what Gianpaolo might come up with was high. Italians are fussy about their kitchens, and I fully expected Gianpaolo to deliver an artistic vision that would rival that of Bernini.

When we visited his shop again, Gianpaolo proudly presented us with his computerized drawing. His plan eliminated the bulky island altogether and used the empty wall as a place for more countertops, cabinets and a chest-height oven which would mean no more bending over to lift heavy pans. It would have a pull-out pantry for storing canned goods, and best of all, there would be a glorious dishwasher—something the old kitchen had lacked—right underneath the oven. The cabinets included all sorts of savvy design features with special places to stow sponges, tall bottles of oil or wine, and special hidden drawers within drawers for silverware. The result would be a kitchen with much more storage space, a feeling of openness, and greater utility, all without expanding the original footprint of the kitchen. We had been right, Gianpaolo had given us his vision with the precision and care that we would never get at an American big box hardware store.

Visiting and revisiting Gianpaolo's showroom, we ultimately settled on a modern looking kitchen with white enameled uppers and lower cabinets in a contrasting light oak. It was a trendy look and perhaps risky for that reason. I might have made the same stylistic mistake my father had made when he lopped off the graceful portico of our Spanish bungalow in L.A. On the other hand, nothing was more classic than white in a kitchen, and besides, I had just seen a kitchen in *Bravacasa* in this style, and it looked fantastic.

One project begat another. Since we were going to the trouble to retile floors and install a new kitchen, Umberto felt it was also the time to reconfigure the house's layout. He wanted to create two bathrooms downstairs, one for guests, the other as an en suite master bathroom. This time, everything would be built-in—closets, bedside tables, armoires, medicine cabinets. The object was to make it all feel simple, seamless and airy. Umberto spent many an evening huddled before the computer in our little study, drawing up a design of exactly what each bathroom would look like. He was in renovation heaven. In the U.S., a renovation of this magnitude would have required at least a year's salary. In Sardinia, it would cost us only a few months' worth of paychecks.

Both of us wanted simplicity. Since we decided long ago not to have kids, we were freed from having to worry about adding nurseries and extra bedrooms and playrooms. Maybe it was just that we were getting older, or maybe it was something about having uprooted one home in exchange for another, or maybe it was the fact that the house itself gave us enough to worry about, but for whatever reason, when it came to appearances, neither one of us wanted to feel trammeled by disorder or excess. The kitchen would be simple and modernist, without the turned wood of our old kitchen. The floors would be seamless stone throughout, and now, we would lose most of the furniture too. My paintings would be the star of this show.

Renovating is a lot like going into labor. New mothers, once the baby is born, allow the memories of the horrible birthing pain to recede. And we had done the same. We had forgotten (or perhaps suppressed) our memories of what a major pain reconfiguring a house could be. But here we were again, for the second time, having to pull every stick of furniture out of the house. Everything was moved out to the veranda, again, as it had been before. Our existing kitchen was dismantled and given to Claudio, who wanted to use it in his own country house. We were glad to see it go to a good home.

This time, Vincenzo was our contractor of choice. He handled smaller jobs than Soldano and focused on more detailed work that involved a decorative touch. He and his partner would be able to handle the job. They first dismantled all the old bathroom fixtures and created a new opening for the bathroom that would become accessible through the master bedroom. Then, Vincenzo created a wall that would divide the master bathroom from the abutting guest bathroom. While so much was happening downstairs, we asked Vincenzo to also install some recessed lights in the kitchen, to help brighten things up.

The meticulous cutting, laying of tile and grouting, took a couple of weeks. Dust from the wet tile saw coated the veranda, along with all of our furniture. Whenever we popped downstairs to see how the work was going, we always felt a lift.

"The house feels so much bigger!" I said to Umberto. "And it feels like there is so much light!"

By the time Vincenzo was done, and after the new kitchen was installed, the house was barely recognizable. It felt very modern and clean, fresh and designed with purpose. Light bounced around to places it never had before. Our style had morphed from quirky and cottagey to classic simplicity. Fortunately, renovation costs in Italy nowhere near approached what they were in Boston, so we could afford this transformation.

We were largely satisfied with how things had turned out. We had created some dramatic changes in our space, and I was slowly learning in my years on the island that the weeds were going to grow no matter what. Acceptance and, let's face it, a certain amount of resignation, ruled the day. Our house had not quite reached the grandeur of the shelter magazines and never would, but it was our creation, a 3-D composition, and to a certain degree we had conquered it. The question was, would we ever feel the same about Sardinia?

"I can't take it anymore!" I screamed at Umberto. "I need more. I don't want to teach, but even if I did, I wouldn't get paid for it here. I'm painting but there's nowhere to exhibit. I can't freelance. I have nothing going on. What am I supposed to do? I can't just make marmalade all day!"

Tears streamed down my face as I paced back and forth on our large lawn. My throat felt so tight I could barely swallow.

"This is where my job is," Umberto retorted, his voice rising in frustration. "We can't just pick up and leave. I don't have any prospects anywhere else."

It was another one of our fights.

We'd been in Sardinia now for several years, spending our time making and remaking the house endlessly, almost obsessively. For a while, it had been enough. There was a lot of satisfaction to be had in shaping and reshaping our immediate environment. And after the house, I had immersed myself in art. I pored over art history books, art magazines, spent many hours in my studio, experimenting while I listened to Italian singers crooning love songs on

Radio Internazionale. It had helped to salve a sense I'd often had of floating unmoored on this island, truly isolated and adrift. But I was getting older and wiser. I now had a much firmer foot in reality and I had finally begun to grasp what I could change, and what I couldn't. To my mind, we had hit the limit. Some of it was the house, and some of it was Sardinia.

As far as the house went, I had slowly developed a love/hate relationship with it. Although I enjoyed the privacy and serenity of having our own place, I had begun to notice that we were dealing with a continual succession of needling problems that other friends and neighbors didn't have. We joked that it was "the curse of Angelo." Every eighteen months, the electrical motor of our well pump started whirring continuously. The *"corrente galvanica"* (or Galvanic current), the electrical charge emanating from our unique soil and water composition, was doing its dirty work corroding a metal part of the well pipe meant to provide just this sort of protective function for the well motor. If we didn't attend to it right away by pulling the whole 72-foot contraption out of the ground, we would burn out the 400 Euro motor. And then there was the irrigation system. It required a Ph.D. to run it. Umberto had a Ph.D., but I didn't, and I struggled with understanding the complex settings and obscure coding. I was impatient, and I had never enjoyed fussing with buttons and settings when a simple turn of a faucet would do. This would be less of an issue if the irrigation system didn't need reprogramming each time the power went down, but it did, and the power went down often, almost daily, due to the fact that our home had not been designed to handle modern-day appliances. If I forgot and turned on the oven at the same time that I did a load of laundry, a fuse would trip, and the house would go dark. Each time this happened, I also had to climb on a rickety chair positioned perilously above the steep stairway into the basement to reset the cistern where our well water collected. One wrong move and I would literally break my neck. And there were other problems. An ugly crack had developed on the kitchen wall, and it opened and closed seasonally, like a concrete lung. After hiring an engineer to investigate, we discovered that part of the house was settling due to the lack of a real foundation. We had to hire a company to come in to blast foam underground just to shore things up. As if all these things weren't bad enough, we also seemed to live in some strange microclimate, which we dubbed "Angelo's vortex." For whatever reason, our plot of land was much windier and stormier than that of neighboring properties only a few meters away. In fact, in a region not known for it, a tornado once ripped very close to our home, barely missing taking off our roof. And once, when Soldano's crew had been working on our guest house, a bolt of lightning had hit their cement mixer, barely missing one of his workers. It was kind of strange. All the storms swirling exclusively around our property meant lots of power outages, water damage, and trees keeling over. This was in addition to the normal problems like the septic tank backing up into the guest house when Umberto's parents visited, or the roof leaking during certain rainstorms, despite our best efforts to fix it. For such a small place, maintaining and attending to all the systems required an engineering degree, which luckily Umberto had, but I majored in journalism. Compared to the simplicity of the house I had grown up in in Los Angeles, it seemed incomprehensibly more complex and I'd found myself feeling less and less at home living there. I had come to realize that if Umberto were to leave on a business trip or fall sick, I would not be able to survive a day on my own.

And then there were our neighbors.

Our house was not a stand-alone house. It was attached to another house divided into two when the original three sisters who owned the land decided to split it up. That meant we were close, far too close, to a family next door who had once owned our property, and therefore imagined that they still owned it. Fortunately, that family used their "house" only in the traditional way, as a shed and a place to throw occasional Sunday afternoon lunches. But still, they came by most every day to work in the garden. The sister who owned the house had a husband, short and cantankerous, who was so disagreeable that we came up with a name for him that held among our family and friends: "The Monster." We gave him this name after a run-in I had with him.

"We need flowers," I said to Umberto one day. "Let's plant some geraniums outside our gate to give the house and the street a little life."

Umberto was all in. Who, after all, could have a problem with flowers?

I spent weeks on my project. First, I lovingly planted small cuttings taken from geraniums inside the garden, with Claudio's help. Claudio showed me how to trim and prepare the cuttings for planting and how far apart to space each plant.

"See, each branch should only be so big," he showed me on his knees, using his pruning shears to create a new sprig for planting. "And they need to go about this distance apart."

I sat in the dirt with him, digging a shallow hole in the dry soil.

Since we had no irrigation in this part of the property, I filled up a large plastic watering can with a garden hose and carried it out beyond the gate under a blistering sun each day for several weeks, carefully watering and tending to my plants. The neighbors across the way saw me out there each afternoon in the blazing heat, and one of them, whom we refer to as "the *poliziotto's* wife" (later we came to know her as Adelaide), nodded approvingly. The geraniums grew beautifully, tall and colorful. In fact, they made a striking statement on our dusty lane, otherwise run over with dry weeds. But the flowers, so beautiful to most of our neighbors, offended *Il Mostro*. He was one of those pigheaded Sardinians of a certain generation who found virtue in being a bullheaded, unyielding stubborn boor. He insisted that my trim row of geraniums took up too much space on a dead-end street in which cars seldom passed. One day, while Umberto was at work, I heard a car door slam, then the roar of a rototiller, very nearby. I looked outside the window, horrified to see The Monster on a tear, razing all my lovingly-planted geraniums to the ground. In a panic, I called Umberto.

"You won't believe what he's doing!" I shrieked in shock. "He's zapping all our flowers!"

I threw down the phone and ran outside to confront The Monster face to face. My Italian was still not good enough to handle the more creative Italian curse words, but I managed with the few standard ones I was familiar with.

"What are you doing?!" I bellowed in disbelief.

"*Signora*, no one can get by," The Monster barked, imperiously. "And I decide what happens on this street. *Io! Comando io!*"

I was stupefied. Somehow, I couldn't see something like this happening in Boston, L.A. or Rome, where civilized people had more important things to do than viciously brutalize a neighbor's flowers. (In Rome, a bike or wallet might get stolen, but there was a sense of purpose in that.) It took me a long time to get over the incident, and I never talked to The Monster again. I was not surprised, years later, when The Monster was arrested for attempting to murder his own son with a hammer. Thankfully, the gun laws were stronger in Italy than in the United States, or we would all be dead.

Sardinia was beautiful, but it could also be rough. I had read Sardinian author Grazia Deledda's novel, *Canne al Vento*, and all the misplaced honor, superstition and barbarism she recounted in 1913 certainly held true 90 years later. I missed the refinement of the city. Seared into my mind for the rest of perpetuity was the sight of a dog whose throat had been slit, blood dripping down his fur, a long tongue lollygagging out the side of his mouth, pendulously suspended from a chain-link fence along one of the main roads leading to our house. No doubt, the unlucky creature had the misfortune to wander into someone's land and threaten the sheep or the chickens. Evidently, some farmer or shepherd had taken care of the matter in a brutal, backwoods way to send a brutal, backwoods message to the dog's owner. It felt like a scene out of *Deliverance*. The savage barbarism of the act shook me to my core, especially being a dog lover.

I had traded in my citified American life for life in the Sardinian countryside, but I had always conceived of Sardinia as a gentle place. Sometimes it was, and sometimes it wasn't. I had nurtured the thought, a fantasy perhaps, that I could carve out some new professional direction for myself doing something needed and necessary among people who would appreciate it. None of that seemed to be the case. For sure I was tired of trying to eke out money from teaching English. One of the worst offenders was the Italian government, which hired me once to teach English to a bunch of loud, obnoxious teenagers attending the island's *Istituto Alberghiero*, the Hospitality School. It was there that one of my male students, a scrawny pockmarked 16-year-old, even had the gall to ask me for my telephone number during a lesson on the conjugation of the verb "to be." I had no idea how to handle these ruffians. I finally called the dean into the classroom to plead for order. And what did I get for all this trouble? Not a *centesimo*. Though I had managed to write a few articles occasionally for some American magazines, for the most part, most American publications did not seem interested in publishing whatever stories I could wrangle out of my Sardinian experiences. And since we lived on an island, it was neither simple nor affordable for me to travel to report on stories anywhere else. Painting had become my passion, but no matter how hard I looked or who I talked to, there was no way to bring my paintings to the world. There were virtually no galleries on my side of the island where I could show, and not much of an artistic community where I might gain some inspiration and support. If painting was my passion, it was destined to remain a private one with my canvases building up in our closets and attic creating the clutter that I so despised. I found that depressing. And then there was the social fabric. I never expected to really "fit in" on an isolated island where the genetic pool had been so limited for so many centuries that a high percentage of the population was prone to odd diseases like favism, a genetic disease leading to anemia upon ingestion of fava beans. I had never become accustomed to the stares I got, even in Alghero, simply because I looked different from everyone else. Children in grocery stores stopped in their tracks when they saw me, mesmerized as if I had two heads. I wanted to yell "boo!" but I didn't.

And then, of course, there was the language. I had initially grasped the very basics of Italian in those early years—the course in Boston and then the first course in Sardinia—and over time I had become accustomed to the most common phrases and exclamations, so I could mostly follow television shows and movies. But I still had come to the language very late, and it showed. I had a painful flat American accent. I could hear it for myself when I struggled to speak, and it grated on my nerves. I was never able to open my mouth to enunciate my vowels and roll my "R's" in that rich round way that Italians did. I'd also never gotten used to using the formal *"lei"* construction, which we didn't have in more egalitarian English. Italians were forgiving of these faults, but I hated that no matter how hard I tried, I made tons of mistakes and people had difficulty understanding what I said. When I spoke, I noticed that listeners took on a pained expression, wincing, as if they were rooting for an underdog. On another level, I felt like I couldn't be myself, since it was hard to be witty, tell jokes or make astute observations when your vocabulary was limited to three words. I was a mute and dull dinner guest.

Umberto was also dealing with roadblocks of his own. Initiatives he had proposed at the university were either very slow to happen or never took off at all. Some of his colleagues had reached a point in their own careers where they were not exactly pushing. In fact, they were barely showing up. Once the lunch hour rolled around, they disappeared, not to be seen for the rest of the day. Needless to say, it was not exactly motivating.

We could decide at this point to put our energies into having children and raising a family, the way everyone else had. But that wasn't the direction that was calling me. We both craved the crazy tumult of the city. We craved opportunity. We craved more stimulation. Maybe not forever. After all, by now, we felt tied to Sardinia. I had learned a lot in this place, about generosity, friendship, the joys of living close to nature and how good *Malloreddus*, a small Sardinian pasta resembling *gnocchi*, could be when seasoned with a dash of saffron and fresh sausage. We didn't want to completely abandon this project in midstream. But we both needed a breather. Though we hadn't come to any sort of agreement about the need for a change, the reality of it hung in the air.

Serendipitously, not long after our exchange in the garden, something happened that would resolve the whole issue: Umberto called one afternoon during an hour in which he was normally teaching. That struck me as odd, but there was excitement in his voice.

"Pam, you won't believe this," he said. "I just got offered a six-month research stint—at Harvard."

HOME # TWO
A CONDO IN BOSTON-
STRATHMORE ROAD

"So, what do you think?" Umberto asked me. "Taking this could be just the break we need."

We were deliberating once more about making a temporary move back to Boston. Umberto was the sort of guy who enthusiastically embraced new projects and adventures, and this would be yet another new adventure. Although he was an engineer with a technical mind, who felt comfortable and even stimulated by the complexities of our house in Sardinia, he also understood my frustration.

"Let's go for it," I told him. "We don't have kids or a reason why we *have* to stay here. It would be nice for both of us to get away for a while. Let's see what happens."

I was excited. I would get to visit friends in Boston, perhaps take a few classes, establish new freelance connections, tap into the vibrancy of city life again. Umberto would be able to network and add a few more lines to his résumé. We weren't giving up on making a home in Sardinia by any means. We were, well, just sort of expanding. And if it was a risk to move to Sardinia in the first place, why not take another to move back to Boston?

I began perusing Boston apartment listings online.

"This is going to be harder than I thought," I said to Umberto one evening after dinner, as I surfed through real estate listings on the internet. "Do you know how much they're asking for rent? At least $1,000! And that's just for a studio! It seems like a waste to spend so much on rent. Besides, all the apartments I've found so far are leasing for a year. And they don't allow pets."

This last factor was perhaps the biggest problem. We were not going to abandon loyal Tony who had made the long journey from Boston to Sardinia. And now we also had a cat, Mattonella, who insisted on her rightful place atop any bed we should own anywhere in the world.

Maybe it seemed like a leap, but I concluded we had to buy. I still had a small nest egg back from my days at *The Globe*, and investments I had made while at the paper were doing well. We could take some of that money and sink it into buying a pied-a-terre in Boston. Our mortgage would still be less than the cost of rent, and at the end of the six months, we would have a sound investment that we could rent out to visiting professors and researchers, of which there was no dearth in Boston. When we needed it from time to time, our savvy little investment could become a cozy escape from the melancholia of Sardinia's desolate winters. And if we ever needed to sell, at the rate at which Boston property appreciated, we could make a tidy little profit.

In the Spring of the following year, during a trip we made to Boston to firm up the details of Umberto's research stint, we made an offer on a one-bedroom condo in Boston's Brighton neighborhood. Just west of the more centralized neighborhoods of the Back Bay and Kenmore Square, and abutting the urban "streetcar" suburb of Brookline, "Allston-Brighton," was once a big stockyard, but had become the home of many students, young professionals living on the cheap while they paid off hefty student loans, and recent immigrants, mostly from Asia, Latin America or Russia.

Our realtor, Connor, a dapper Irishman with an Irish brogue, had shown us a grand total of three apartments—the amount in our low price range that we were able to see on the last Friday we were in town. The one that caught our eye was of a modest size—only 650 square feet. It was in a 1920s art deco building, a quiet top floor corner unit, overlooking backyards and gardens. The layout was a good one, with the bedroom and bathroom tucked away from the entry and kitchen, the way we liked. The unit didn't have a dining room, but the foyer was large enough to accommodate a desk, which could be converted into a small dining table when we needed it. There was even a roof deck in the building. Somehow, we managed to get a mortgage, despite the fact that I didn't have a job and Umberto's income was earned in Italy, not in the United States. The bank insisted that I write a letter stating that I expected to make in the U.S. the exact same salary I made in Sardinia. That was easy. I didn't make a salary in Sardinia, and I wasn't counting on making one in Boston, either. I was speedily approved for a loan.

Anxious to make a deal quickly and grab a place that stood out among the three student rat traps we had seen, we offered just under full price on a Friday night, hoping to entice the seller to accept our offer before the first open house was held on Sunday. Our Irish realtor was also the realtor for the owner, and he had a vested interest in closing this deal quickly before any other realtor could muscle in on his commission.

"Why not wrap up the deal before the open house, so you don't even have to bother?" he cajoled the owner. "You don't have any guarantee you'll get another offer, so best to take one you have in hand for nearly full asking price, you see. And the unit needs some work, after all. This is a good price."

And to us, he said, "If she has an open house *anything* might happen. A bidding war might break out, you see. The unit is in great shape. Much better than the others we looked at. Better to offer your best and final offer straight away!"

We knew he was playing both sides of the fence, but we didn't care. We needed a place to live, and we needed it fast. Our offer and his ploy worked. The owner accepted and canceled the open house.

A couple of months later, we moved in. Or rather *I* moved in. Umberto and Tony remained in Sardinia. I slept on a blow-up mattress on the floor, borrowed a truck from my friend Greg, and embarked on the pressing task of finding a bed and couch and table and silverware. The apartment was so small, fortunately, that it didn't take long to get what we needed.

We owned the apartment on Strathmore Road for far longer than we ever expected to. The first time I walked in after the closing, I was surprised by what bad shape the place was in. *We actually bought this dump?* The former owner had obviously never thought to take a paintbrush to the walls or even to replace a missing cover on the fluorescent light fixture in the kitchen. The wooden floors were worn and scratched. Some of the ancient windows were jammed closed, unusable. In the years that we owned it, a lot changed.

We repainted the grayed walls and hired a zealous crew of Brazilians, none of whom spoke a word of English, to gut renovate the bathroom and remove the uneven popcorn ceiling. Mostly that went smoothly.

But one day, in the midst of the whacking and whomping of hammers and crowbars, I suddenly heard a workman shriek in alarm "*Meu Deus! Meu Deus!*" I ran into the bathroom to find the youngest Brazilian on his knees desperately trying to cover a hole in a pipe with his bare hands. A violent torrent of water spewed everywhere, onto floors and walls and fixtures. The water was rising quickly, and it wouldn't be more than a few minutes before it swept through the entire apartment. There was a look of panic, perhaps terror, on the young Brazilian's face. I leaped for the phone to call the property manager.

"Turn off the water, turn off the water!" I screamed into the phone. Eventually, that did happen, but not before all three floors of apartments directly beneath us got flooded, destroying many ceilings and floors. So much water gushed out of that pipe that water made it all the way down into the storage room on the first floor of the four-story building. Fortunately, the Brazilian contractor assured us that he could take care of repairing all of it, which he did.

Aside from that debacle, all the other changes we made went smoothly. We replaced the doors of the kitchen cabinets, installed a skylight in the darkened foyer that I used as a home office, and installed new windows. The new vinyl windows functioned better than the original ones from 1925, although they did not approach the efficient design of the sturdy Italian windows we had installed in our house in Sardinia. Umberto had long lamented the fact that American standards for such things were far lower than Italian standards. We, of course, replaced the broken light fixture in the kitchen, although again, we couldn't find anything of interesting design and good quality. In Boston, we lived in a Home Depot kind of world—bland, standardized, devoid of quality or originality. We made do with our limited choices and still managed to fashion a perfect cozy winter hideout. As the steam radiators gurgled and hissed, successfully staving off the icy temperatures outside, I reveled in how much warmer the Boston apartment was in comparison to the house in Sardinia. The toasty warmth inside our little apartment managed to make Boston's brutal winters tolerable. I also noticed that despite the extensive renovations we had done, the small condo's contained spaces were much easier to deal with than the Alghero house. Things happened faster, and small changes seemed to have a much bigger impact. On so many levels, life in a condo was so much simpler than life in a house. In a couple of weeks, we had totally renovated the place, and it would forever be the better for it. In Sardinia, if you graveled the driveway, you could rest assured that within a few months' time, you would need to gravel again. But the city apartment didn't have a driveway and the condo association worried about maintaining the exterior. There were no wells to worry about, no septic tanks, no irrigation systems. Here, we were free of Angelo's Curse.

As the apartment got renewed and refreshed, so did our respective careers. I took on a lucrative freelance contract writing for a large hospital chain. I wrote web stories on health topics like heart disease, obesity, and insomnia. The work paid well but didn't require a lot of time, and I was able to spend much of my time in painting and drawing classes and attending lectures and exhibits. In that period, my art seemed to have been informed by all my time in Sardinia. I was painting large abstracts in organic colors—rich terra cotta hues and deep greens. I reconnected with many of my old friends from *The Globe*, and we regularly exchanged *Globe* gossip over dinner. I also made new friends in the drawing and paintings classes I attended several times a week. I felt my world opening up like a flower, moving beyond the intense domestic focus it had had in Sardinia. In this period in Boston, I walked down the street smiling to myself, a bounce in my step, because it felt as if I had pulled off a rare feat. Expanding our place of residence to go global had worked. Somehow, I had managed to have a little bit of everything—Europe and the U.S., tradition, and novelty, freedom, and security—creativity in all realms. I had a life of choices. Most people, whether they lived in Italy or the United States, weren't so lucky. Umberto, meanwhile, was able to transform his research stint into a long-term collaboration where we could be assured of having a reason to return to Boston a few months out of each year, at least for a while. He, too, had somehow dodged the bullet of conventionality.

We watched our real estate risk pay off too. Housing prices continued to ascend well beyond the affordable, and when we weren't staying there, the apartment on Strathmore Road never lacked for renters. We fell into a pattern in which I spent September through February in Boston and Umberto joined me in November, after his own school year was over in Sardinia, until the end of January, when he returned to Italy. I joined him a month later. It was a pattern carefully devised to take advantage of the best of what each place had to offer. In Sardinia, the Springtime commotion and clamor of planning and planting the garden moved into languorous summer days at the beach, hiking trips and backyard barbecues. But by the end of September, with the days growing shorter, a sense of desolation and ennui set in. When the November rainy season came, the backyard became muddy, the house became cold and humid, and there wasn't much happening in town. In Boston, on the other hand, September signaled the beginning of new life. Students returned, artists opened their studios, musicians, and actors prepared for the fall entertainment season. There was a feeling of excitement and possibility as palpable as the bright red and orange leaves on the trees. On the other hand, by March, I was sick of Boston's cold, sick of piling on hats, gloves, and parkas to leave the house, sick of the sick and tired dour Bostonians. I missed how good-looking the Italians were, how well-dressed they were. They were always a pleasure to look at. In Boston, by contrast, I mostly averted my eyes from the pasty, puffy sea of humanity around me. I was always eager to get back to the warm and pleasant breezes of Sardinia and its sense of earthiness and connection. Boston could be stimulating, but I missed the sense of community and common good that threaded through life in Europe. While people in Italy meticulously collected their food waste for collection, while they bought efficient light bulbs and avoided palm oil out of concern for deforestation in Borneo, Americans were still carelessly barreling down highways in giant Hummers. I wanted to get back to common sense.

We managed our back-and-forth lifestyle just fine.

Then September 11th happened.

When jets slammed into the Twin Towers, the happy ease of our globe-trotting lifestyle came crashing down with a loud rumble of finality.

The day it happened, I was napping on the couch of our *salotto* in Alghero. A fantastic summer was winding down. Soon, I would be returning to Boston for an exhibit of my paintings. As I napped, birds chirped, and a beautiful late summer sunlight filtered through our large sliding glass doors. Suddenly, the phone rang, disturbing the idyllic peace. It was Umberto calling, overwrought from the office.

"Turn on the TV! Turn on the TV!" he yelled into the phone.

Awakened from my untroubled *pisolino*, I switched on the TV and watched in stunned horror as a large plane plowed into the glass-paneled side of a skyscraper. New Yorkers, dazed and dusted in silt and powder, wandered across the screen. After a couple of minutes, the skyscraper, which we all knew to be filled with people, imploded on itself. I sat down on the couch. My mind couldn't process the enormity of it all.

In this moment, our lives imploded as well. It was no longer so easy for us, unmarried as we were, to spend time living in two countries without the permanent residency conferred by marriage. It was harder for me to stay in Italy as an American citizen and was certainly harder for Umberto to stay in the U.S. as an Italian citizen. Suspicion clouded all travel. After September 11, when Umberto entered the U.S., he was subjected to barking immigration officers, red-faced and irresolute, who wielded seemingly unlimited authority to deride, detain and otherwise torment, as they saw fit. (The immigration officers in Boston were especially angry and derisive, which we attributed to the fact that one of the planes felling the Twin Towers had originated from Boston's Logan Airport.) Somehow, we needed to fix the situation in this ugly new world. And the easiest, most elegant way to fix things would be to do the one thing we hadn't yet done: get married. If Umberto were to obtain a green card, the immigration authorities would still be barking bullies, but maybe they would mitigate their cruelest instincts. It would be a little harder to treat a permanent resident like a piece of trash blown in by the wind, the way they routinely did with tourist and visa holders.

We loved each other, but in the eight years we had been together, neither of us had ever felt we needed a piece of paper to call our relationship legitimate. Now, however, the tenor of the times demanded it.

When I had married thirteen years earlier, I had been fresh out of college, untraveled, and to some degree, naïve. Now I was older. I had lived with three men, and one of them was dead. Although I was not afraid of taking the plunge again, it was no longer a priority. Weddings, ceremony, pieces of paper, were no protection against life. To my mind, Umberto and I could live together happily, create our own brand of family and a home, and it didn't require anything more official than our happiness and dedication to each other.

On his end, Umberto was used to the European way in which couples often lived together without ever feeling the need to marry. It's true, back in Brookline, in those first few months, Umberto *had* proposed to me by sending Tony into the room with a box holding an emerald ring tied around his neck. It was his way of showing he understood the gravity of me quitting my job to move to Italy, (and it helped legitimize the whole move for both my parents and Umberto's conservative Catholic mother.) But that ring had been enough for us.

While Italians, especially those from the village, might have had a big ceremony involving half the village, they seemed to hold fewer illusions about what followed after the pomp and circumstance. (Plus, they had the good sense not to embarrass themselves by asking bridesmaids to wear preposterous ruffled pastel dresses.) Weddings were less commercialized and often far simpler than American ceremonies held on the beach or in a hot air balloon. Marriage itself was less about fantasy and more about cold, hard reality. Now, setting our own sentiments aside, we had cold, hard reality staring us in the face. If we finally got married, we would eliminate all the problems we faced as a couple living in two countries in a post 9-11 world.

"We're going to have to get married," I said to Umberto. "Life would be so much simpler."

"*Sono d'accordo*," Umberto said.

"But I don't want to do it the way I did it before," I said. "I don't want a lot of show and stress, the complications of long-distance travel for two families spread around the globe. Lyle and Kendra spent more than $40,000 on theirs. I think that's crazy. I want something simple, meaningful, uncomplicated, and fun."

Suddenly, an idea popped into my head.

"I have it! I turned to Umberto, excitedly. "Let's do what one of my co-workers once did at *The Globe*. Let's invite a few people over, have a catered dinner, and surprise everyone by getting married!"

"*Mitico*!" exclaimed Umberto.

The idea appealed to Umberto's sense of whimsy. The Italians might call it *spiritoso* although most Italians would never have the courage to plan any kind of union without *mamma* and the rest of the *famiglia*.

On a cold day in March, when the sun shone bright, but snow still covered delicate spring crocuses, we organized a dinner at a friend's house—an elegant apartment in Boston's Back Bay. The apartment belonged to our friend Sabine and overlooked the Charles River. The ostensible reason for the dinner was to celebrate Umberto's recent promotion from assistant professor to associate professor. That explained why we were both wearing outfits we would never ordinarily wear, especially in March. Umberto was wearing a jacket, something he never did, and I was wearing silver sandals and a white sleeveless chiffon dress with big splashy flowers. Ordinarily, this time of year, I would be wearing jeans, a sweater, and boots. I froze between the cab and Sabine's front door. Inside, Sabine's apartment had been elegantly outfitted for the occasion. A large oval table draped in an elegant white tablecloth had been placed next to the window with a view of the Charles and, beyond that, Cambridge. Flowers adorned the table. The lights of MIT twinkled and winked, as if they were in on the secret. Twelve of our friends arrived. As we sat around the table, and the caterers brought us our first course of pumpkin soup followed by a main course of pork medallions, my friend Greg, who knew about our plans and who would be marrying us, initiated a conversation.

"So," he asked casually, "are you guys ever going to get married?"

The table immediately broke into jovial conversation. Our friends were in rare form with their good-natured ribbing.

"Yeah," rejoined Alessandro, as if on cue. It had not taken much to ignite his teasing. He liked to provoke controversy whenever there was the opportunity. "How many years have you been together anyway?

The others picked right up on theme, like a chorus in a Greek play, providing all the appropriate repartee to keep the thread of the conversation moving in the right direction. They thought they were tormenting us, but it was just what we were hoping for.

"It must be at least ten years," said Marianne, the friend who rescued me that summer after Phil's death.

"What are you waiting for?" added Alessandro's boyfriend, Daniel.

As everyone continued along with their ripostes and wit, what Greg had to say after a while seemed quite natural.

"Well, Pam, would you ever accept Umberto as your lawful wedded husband?" he posited. There was a pause.

"Yes, I would," I responded, looking into Umberto's eyes.

"And would you, Umberto, accept Pam as your lawful wedded wife?" Greg asked.

"Sure, I would," replied Umberto, looking into my eyes.

"Wait." said Greg. "Does anyone have any rings?"

My friend Sabine jumped up. She had been waiting for her part in this play.

"Yes, I think I have something here in this drawer," she cooed solicitously. She opened a nearby drawer, pulling out two rings in a little white box. She took out the rings, simple bands of white gold that we bought at a jewelry store in downtown Alghero and handed them to Greg as if they were some stray paper clips she had casually found in a drawer. Greg gave them to us to slip on each other's fingers.

Everyone looked on, spellbound, but somehow not quite catching on.

"Well," said Greg dramatically, pulling a marriage certificate out of his front pocket, "with the power invested in me by the state of Massachusetts, I now pronounce you man and wife!"

The table was stunned. "Whoa! What? Did you guys just get married?" Marianne asked.

Yes, we told her. We did.

"You did not!" she said. She snatched the marriage certificate out of Greg's hands and scanned it suspiciously. Some friends laughed. Our friend Giusi began to cry. And Alessandro, mischievous Italian provocateur that he was, well, he was mad.

"If I knew you were getting married," he scolded, "I would have dressed better!"

HOME # THREE
A CONDO IN BOSTON—
ALLSTON STREET

"We need more space!" I said to Umberto.

I was sorting through art supplies stacked on a cart in the corner of the small apartment we had bought in Boston. Paint brushes jammed old coffee cans that threatened to topple from their precarious perch atop the cart. Mountains of canvases spilled out from behind a bookcase. I had put down a drop cloth to catch splashes underneath a paint-encrusted easel and together, the whole set up loomed over the living room. To make matters worse, friends were coming to stay for the weekend, and we had no place to put them. They would be relegated to the futon in the midst of all the chaos.

"If we had a second bedroom, that could become my studio," I moaned, using my whiny voice designed to express maximum unhappiness. "It makes more sense than paying so much to rent a separate studio."

In fact, I had rented a studio space in Boston's South End for a couple of years as my painting career expanded. I shared it with two painter friends of mine, Timothy and Kathleen, and we made a point of opening our studio to the public every first Friday of the month where we displayed our souls on the wall for everyone to see. I was painting larger works and finding places to exhibit, but I had also discovered that being a serious artist required not only guts, but space, and lots of it, for art supplies, unfinished canvases, and at least a little bit of room to set up paintings when galleries came to visit. The 50 square feet in the corner of our 650 square foot apartment just wasn't enough. The rented loft near downtown had been a solution, but it was expensive, about the price of renting a live-in unit. I had also found it inconvenient to cross town with art supplies and canvases on Boston's creaky subway system. Listening to one of Boston's trains strain down the tracks was similar to hearing nails scrape across a blackboard. Who wanted to hear that every day if there was a way to avoid it?

I pulled out my calculator and did the math. A two-bedroom apartment would cost us roughly $50,000 to $100,000 more. As a practical matter, that added cost would still add up to less of a monthly expense than renting a studio on my own, and there wouldn't be the added hassle of having to commute across town.

That's it, we agreed. We needed a bigger apartment.
Our list of needs was short and looked like this:
Two bedrooms
Within a short walk of a T stop
An extra space that could serve as a guest room
Lots and lots of light

An association that allowed pets

We had a list of "wants" too—an open floor plan that would feel spacious and loft-like, a dining room where we might finally entertain, zero wasted space. But we were willing to compromise on those if we found something in our price range meeting our list of needs.

In Sardinia, we spent our Sunday mornings biking around in search of shelter magazines. In Boston, our Sundays were spent visiting open houses. I loved inspecting other people's houses almost as much as I loved opening the latest edition of a new decorating magazine. After a few months of scavenging through the tangled thicket of Boston housing, we ventured to a nearby open house where we met Matt. He was a balding, mild-mannered, gently affable realtor, a former economist who lived in Japan for a while and spoke fluent Japanese. We weren't interested in the apartment he was selling, but after spending some time talking with him, we decided to hire him as our agent. We were taken in by his relaxed, non-predatory air, a distinct rarity among real estate agents. From that point on, with and without him, we saw dozens upon dozens of apartments, all old, usually defective in some blatant way. Even so, desperate to move as we watched housing prices march inexorably upward, we made a bid on quite a few of them. Every time we finally stumbled across something we loved (or at least could accept) we made an offer only to have the whole scene flare into a conflagration of warring bids. It was as if we had been cursed.

One week in spring, as bulbs nudged out of garden beds and leaves erupted on trees, an ad appeared on the MLS advertising a condo not too far from our own in Brighton. We had originally confined our search to Brookline, which boasted decent public transportation, leafy and safe streets, a walkable town center and a certain feel of stability, most likely due to the fact that it was filled with the well-to-do. We wanted to break out of transient and trashier Brighton. But after two years of looking, it was clear we couldn't compete in tony Brookline, where the police had been known to be called on wild turkeys or when someone had glimpsed smoke spewing from, of all things, a chimney. Brookline commanded a premium due to its good schools. Accepting that reality, we began to look outside of Brookline, and nearby Brighton kept popping up as an alternative. A condo in Brighton, comparable in size with one in Brookline, ran an average of $100,000 to $150,000 less.

"Feels like Beacon Hill in Brookline" the listing had gushed. Doubtfully, I set off for the open house alone. Umberto was in Italy. Matt was busy fielding some other open house. My first impression was of a neighborhood that was clearly not Beacon Hill, nor Brookline, either, for that matter. Bits of milk carton and plastic water bottles littered nearby streets and alleys. It was not enough to be considered filthy, but just enough to lend the area a piquant grit. Graffiti smeared nearby walls. There were several senior and low-income housing projects nearby, which helped give the area a big-city "New York" feel but without the glamour of say Williamsburg or Bed-Stuy. The people on the street were mostly in their 20s—students and graduate students attending local colleges. They traveled the streets in packs on that Sunday morning, in search of a fortifying breakfast after a night of carousing in local bars.

The building itself was one of Boston's typical old red brick buildings. It was about 110 years old and clearly had not received the love and attention that a tony Beacon Hill building might have. At one time it had been an apartment building, but sometime in the 1980s was converted over to condos and had since largely been re-converted back to rentals, as individual owners moved on to the more promising suburbs but held onto their former homes as lucrative investments. Unsurprisingly, the building reflected the heavy presence of renters. Common areas were nicked and scratched. Carpets were worn. The laundry room consisted of a couple of washing machines sitting on an uneven and cracked concrete floor with plenty of holes and dents in the drywall patched up with duct tape.

In short, the neighborhood was okay but not great. The building was not great but tolerable. However, even with all that, it was the apartment itself that took me by surprise. Clearly, the owners, with only modest success, had spent some time trying to create an appealing home. They had humbly renovated the kitchen and bathroom a few years earlier. They had repainted and selected fixtures and furniture in what I called "traditional colonial Home Depot," hence the realtor's reference to Beacon Hill. The décor wasn't our style, and the apartment itself didn't quite have the "sex appeal" that others we had seen had, but the bones were good. It sat on a corner with a Southeast exposure. It offered two bedrooms well-separated from each other. The largest could be a perfect painting studio. It had a sunroom right off the dining room, just large enough for a desk and a couch—a perfect home office and occasional guest room. It had a kitchen that opened onto the dining room. This would be good for entertaining. There were lots of windows—21 to be precise—and even a balcony right off the living room large enough to allow for summer meals outside. There were no long hallways or oversized foyers—not even one square foot of wasted space. And to boot, there were loads of architectural details, including crown molding, chair rails, French doors, wall molding, recently polished wood floors. In short, it was more than a pied-a-terre. It felt like a home.

I brought Alessandro and Daniel over to see it. I could tell by the looks on their faces that they thought I was crazy.

"I hope you're going to do something about that," said Daniel, pointing to the ceiling that sagged and bulged like breasts on a South Boston dowager.

In the state it was in, it took imagination, or perhaps desperation, to see all the potential. Of course, I had plans to redo the sagging ceiling. But aside from that, there was one other glaring defect that bothered me even more than the ceiling: the wall.

The wall separated a very long, narrow, and dark living room, from the dining room and kitchen. The dining room and kitchen caught all the morning light. The living room had virtually no light, as it was dependent on windows underneath a covered balcony on the far end. In addition, the wall had two very awkward doorways, one leading to the kitchen, one leading to the dining room, and they abutted each other. At one time in the apartment's history, there had been a wall separating the kitchen from the dining room, which explained the two doorways. It took no imagination at all to see that knocking down the wall between the narrow living room and open kitchen and dining room would totally change the character of the apartment. In one fell swoop, we could open up the entire apartment to light and views and air, and eliminate the redundant doorways, creating one logical large passage with columns and a low bookshelf that could also house the TV. If we made this bold move, not only would we give the apartment a more modern feel and increased functionality, but we could also respectfully maintain all the original period detail in the apartment. In fact, a new opening with woodwork to match the existing woodwork would better befit the original grandeur with which the apartment had been conceived. This would not be one of those renovations that would cause later owners to ask themselves, *"What were they thinking?"*

And besides, we'd been through all this before. This renovation was just another crack at refining our idea of home. This time, it was not just a redo of a pied-a-terre, it was a chance to create an urban paradise, just as we had attempted to create a rural one in Sardinia.

Although Umberto was in Italy, I faxed him the floor plan. He was a floor-plan kind of guy. Whereas I relied on photos to get the "feel" of a place, he looked only at layouts, cold hard paper and the concrete brass-tack reality of square meters (or feet in this case.) Without photos, he could see how a revised floor plan could make this apartment work, and he didn't need photos to discern an apartment's charm and character, the way I did.

"Go for it," he said. I had seen the apartment by myself on Sunday afternoon, but by Sunday evening, I had called Matt and asked him to draw up an offer. Afraid of losing yet another place, we made our offer very close to the owner's asking price. This time, most likely because it was Brighton and not sought-after Brookline, we won.

"Did we offer too much?" I kept asking Umberto anxiously. We had been used to bidding in competitive Brookline, but maybe Brighton was different. Maybe we had offered way too much for a place that needed so much work.

"No, it was the right price," Umberto reassured me. "It's clearly the best thing we've seen, the layout is really very good, and we really didn't want to risk losing it after two years of looking. We did the right thing."

Umberto always seemed convinced that whatever move we made, it was the right thing.

As soon as we closed on the sale, we got down to our dusty business. We hired Walt, the boyfriend of a friend, to knock down the load-bearing wall separating the dining room from the living room. Like Soldano working on the Sardinian house, he would need to replace the wall with a beam (this time wooden) to prevent the entire apartment building from collapsing into one big heap. Part of the renovation would include entirely removing the sagging plaster ceiling and replacing it with a tight, white new ceiling complete with recessed lights. And of course, we would finish up with a bright, light coat of paint throughout the entire apartment.

The renovation happened fast and furiously, and it seemed much easier than Sardinia had been. There were no concrete walls to bust through and simply less material involved in demolition. It was fortunate because we needed to get in by the end of the month since we had quickly sold the Strathmore condo and set a closing date.

Within two weeks, there was a stark transformation.

With the wall gone, it was undeniable that we had done the right thing. This was what this space had cried out for, unheard and desperate in its despair. Yes, it took a lot of effort and money and dust. Yes, there would have been few willing to go to the expense in a building like this, in a neighborhood like this. But the feeling of having finally conquered the brutal housing market to find a place that met all of our criteria and more (a grocery store was conveniently located right across the street) was wonderful. Our apartment, the changes we had made, left an impression. When friends came to visit, they inevitably exclaimed, "cool space!" Once, a fireman responding to a call about a possible gas leak in the building took pains to tell me, "Got a nice place!" as fumes wafted through the hallways. We were satisfied and happy. We had done what obviously needed to be done and we had more space. It felt good—at least for the moment.

HOME # FOUR
AN APARTMENT IN ROME—
COLLE OPPIO

You would think we would have been happy. We had a place in Sardinia, a lovely country retreat, quiet and removed from the chaos of the city. We had an adorable little condo in Boston, right in the heart of the American version of Firenze. But of course, we weren't happy. Who ever is?

"Things are not good in the department," Umberto said to me one day. We were back in Sardinia, on one of our favorite hikes to an overlook called Punta Giglio. The walk took us along the coast, past hidden coves, through dry Mediterranean brush, dense forests and eventually high up to a cliff where we stood atop a defense tower left over from World War II. Glints of sunlight on the deep blue sea were so bright it nearly blinded us. Ahead ran Oliver, a basset-hound mix we had adopted following the sad demise of our loyal, happy-go-lucky Tony a few years back. I was relaxed but kept my eyes trained on the forest. The area was populated by wild boar. In fact, it wasn't so far from here that I encountered that wild boar with

Trisha in the woods. Whenever I thought about it while out on the trail, I felt the hairs on my neck stand up.

When we reached the lookout tower, Oliver, curious about what the grown-ups were doing, jumped up on his hind legs resting his front paws on a low stone wall so that he, too, could take in the sea view.

"There's no space to build anything," Umberto went on about his job. His footsteps were heavy along the gravel path. He looked tired.

"I'm an engineer, but I'm in the medical school, and it's hard to attract graduate students in engineering. I think it would be better for me in Rome where I can work in a structure dedicated to the kind of research I do. And I think you'd be happier in Rome too. There's so much going on there. You'd be able to show. You would find more work writing. You'd have *way* more options."

And it was true, I enjoyed Rome whenever we visited. It was lively and sophisticated, artsy but also world-weary in the way of a woman who wakes up wearing make-up she had worn to a party the night before. There were a broader range of "types," meaning that for me, I could be whoever or whatever I wanted. On the other hand, Rome was also chaotic, smoggy and dirty. Whenever we returned to Sardinia after a trip to the city, I always felt a new appreciation for gentle Sardinian breezes infused with the cleansing scent of rosemary.

Why did our lives seem always in flux? Why couldn't we find a home and then stick to it? Years ago, I had left Boston in search of adventure, but I was also under the impression that I was putting down roots. Somehow, in Sardinia, those roots never seemed to quite take.

"I'm willing to try it," I said to Umberto. Why I should agree to this plan made no sense, given the fact that we would then be living in a grand total of three places at once. But I knew Sardinia was not the most natural fit for two city slickers. And while we had built a second urban home in Boston, where we had friends and professional ties, we had not experienced together urbanity in an Italian context. Umberto was used to it, since he was from Rome, but for me it would be a curtain opening on a whole new window of Italy.

A few weeks following this conversation, Umberto was able to cleverly engineer a temporary position in Rome at an Institute dedicated to Sports Science. This would give him an opportunity to assess whether the grass was truly greener on the other side of the fence—a fence we always seemed to be wistfully peering over.

And so, we began hunting for an apartment to lease. I was a little skeptical about this whole thing working out, but Umberto was determined. It seemed to make sense to sign a traditional three-year-lease, even though it was just a temporary position, because Umberto's parents lived in Rome and we often passed through. No matter how things turned out with the job, renting an apartment each month would cost us a fraction of what a few nights in a hotel room would, and with Umberto's family in town, we were bound to pass through frequently. Even if we returned to living in Sardinia full-time, we reasoned, we could keep the Rome apartment as another pied-a-terre.

"We're looking for an apartment in Rome," Umberto announced to all our friends and his colleagues. "It doesn't need to be large, just something downtown." As usual, he was optimistic and unconcerned about taking on this extra financial burden.

Word spread. Umberto told his two brothers—both of whom lived and worked in Rome. He told Zio Bruno and Zia Marzia. He told Giuseppe and Luisa, from high school. And he told his university colleagues, Quirico and

Danilo. Miraculously, after very little time had passed, we discovered that one of his Sardinian colleagues, Signor Micello, a retired professor at his university, had an apartment in Rome to rent and was, at that very moment, searching for a tenant *affidabile*, very important in Italy because of the "three plus two" year leases, meaning that in theory, a lease could run for up to 5 years before being renewed. It felt like fate. Out of thin air, the apartment materialized. We snapped it up. We came *"raccomandati"* since professors tended to only trust other professors.

It didn't take us long to understand how fortunate we really were. It was on the top floor of a *palazzo signorile*, an Italian term indicating an impressively elegant building, usually built during the early 20th century. The Italian epoch for these buildings was known as *Umbertino*. These were apartments built for the bourgeoisie, complete with grand, arched, carriage-sized entrances. It was very close to the Colosseum and even closer to the ruins of Roman emperor Nero's palace. The Santa Maria Maggiore Basilica was just down the street, housing in one of its reliquaries wood said to be derived from the crib of Jesus Christ. So was Rome's other grand Basilica, San Giovanni in Laterano. In other words, it was downtown, but still far enough from the tourist enclaves to enjoy quiet at night. And just as the neighborhood was originally conceived and built for the elite, it remained somewhat so, even as more and more immigrants from China, Africa, and Bangladesh took up residence in stately but crumbling apartments around the borders of Piazza Vittorio Emanuele. The few blocks surrounding our building were, in American terms, a sort of cross between West L.A. and the Upper West Side, although considerably dirtier than both. Paolo Sorrentino, director of the 2014 award-winning film *La Grande Bellezza (The Great Beauty* in

English), shopped at our local supermarket. We saw him once, out with his wife, child, and even the family dog. Actor Willem Dafoe lived one block away and we happened upon him too, happily carrying grocery bags on his way home for dinner. Our local restaurants were frequented by people who would normally never enter our sphere—Italian television personalities, "show" women with plump remade fish lips, politicians, rumpled yet smug. When we walked Oliver in the Colle Oppio Park overlooking the Colosseum, our dog-owning companions were costume designers, theatre critics, musicians, painters, eminent writers, and thinkers. We lived amid the creative intellectual set, and we relished it. It was nothing at all like living in Sardinia.

The apartment itself was a different matter. It had many architectural advantages. It boasted thirteen-foot ceilings and chandeliers clad in gold leaf. The original floors were fashioned out of *graniglia di marmo*, a highly-prized type of flooring in Italy, evolving from the Venetian *terrazzo*, composed of marble bits floating in a lime paste. The beauty of these floors was that they could be laid out in clever patterns and varying colors. Although our floor's pattern and color seemed a little less clever than others, I tried to appreciate what I could of it.

But the space was awkward. It came outfitted in cheap laminate furniture from the 1970s (as with Sardinia, the apartment came partially furnished). Every room was tethered to a large and useless central corridor, a typical Italian layout, which awkwardly sliced the entire apartment in half. At one time before air-conditioning this had facilitated ventilation. Now, aside from isolating the kitchen, making for rather lonely dinner preparations, the hallway demanded perpetual cleaning. The apartment's two long, narrow bathrooms were not only dated but dysfunctional. The shower stall in the largest bathroom was so small it was difficult to even raise an arm to soap up. Every time I tried, the soap rack clattered to a corner of the shower cabin. Calcium deposits stained the old 60s era tiles and had also collected in the pipes, causing the shower to waver cruelly between hot and cold.

"Umberto," I would shriek, wet and soapy in the shower stall. "Do something!"

On cue, Umberto would amble over to the hot water heater above the refrigerator in the kitchen, rotating the gray knob to a tiny drawing, in red, of water pouring from a faucet.

"Okay, that's better!"

The scene was part of our daily routine.

We had reshaped our Sardinian home as we had reshaped our lives. In Boston, we had done the same. Both projects were proof of what could be done with a little determination. But Rome was different. If we owned the place, we fantasized, we would knock down walls and open the kitchen to the living room, using space from an unnecessarily large closet to create light, views, and space for dining. We would eliminate the obnoxiously oversized hallway and create a new layout which would give each bedroom its own artfully designed bathroom and even allow for a third bedroom. The kitchen played an enormous role in our fantasies. It would be right in the mix of things, communicative with the salon, sleekly modern in the Italian way. There would be light. There would be space. There would be intelligence. Scenes of something airy and sophisticated played like a continuous loop film reel in our heads.

However, that was all just a fantasy. The reality was that our Rome apartment wasn't ours to renovate. And so, uncharacteristically, we did nothing. This, alone, was a challenge for me. I had been known to hang artwork in a freshly painted room before the paint was dry.

After a few months in Rome, Umberto realized he didn't want the Rome job.

"There's no room to grow," he said.

We held onto the apartment, though, and used it for getaway weekends and as a place to stay during family visits. When Umberto's mother was diagnosed with pancreatic cancer, we used it more often. Eventually, Umberto's mother passed away, Umberto's father moved to the town he grew up in, about an hour and a half from Rome. Umberto's youngest brother moved to Torino, leaving just one older brother in the city. There were fewer and fewer reasons to pass through town, but we chose not to give up the place. We had developed friendships in the neighborhood over the years, thanks to our daily walks with Oliver. We had become friends with Besmir, a mercurial Albanian painter who told us sad stories of tortured love involving his girlfriend in New York who he had gotten pregnant. We attended his art openings and ate dinner in his little paint-stained atelier owned by an order of Franciscan nuns. We met Lucia, a gravel-voiced theatre critic for RAI—the national radio station—who, when she wasn't chain-smoking, was out dining with very large groups of friends. Anytime she knew we were in town, she invited us to an intimate late-night dinner at the little trattoria on the corner with twelve of her closest friends. We also became friends with Aurora, a professor, and her girlfriend Martina, a fashion designer. While Aurora studied microbes, Martina created tiny bikinis held together only by creatively tied knots. Alessia lived across the street. With hair dyed tomato red, she was a fashionable, Hepburn-esque figure whose two very small dachshunds became best friends with Oliver. We liked the creative, semi-bohemian feel of all of this. It would be difficult to find another apartment at the price we were paying in such a central location, and we would never find such an interesting collection of friends. It felt like, if not a second home, definitely a third one.

To offset the cost, we decided to sublet a bedroom which would help justify the luxury of holding onto a place we seldom used. A succession of "roommates" passed through. There was Tamara from Venezuela, Susan the Scot, Simona, the Italian woman with the English boyfriend, and John the Australian farmer. They were a great help financially, but it also meant the apartment was largely abandoned to unintentionally neglectful roommates who never deigned to treat the apartment with the same care we did. Fortunately, there was never any real damage, until that is, we rented to an Italian congresswoman with two cats.

The congresswoman was referred to us by Martina, who happened to know she was looking for a temporary place to stay while she finished up renovations on her own apartment. She stayed for just two months and informed us that by the time we returned to the apartment, she would be long gone. We returned to Rome early one morning on a direct flight from Boston. We took the train in from Fiumicino and walked the few blocks from Stazione Termini to our place.

"Wasn't that Lorena?" I asked Umberto. I had seen a woman carrying bags and suitcases out of the corner of my eye. At first, I had assumed it was just another one of Rome's legions of homeless who squatted in the streets in our neighborhood. But no, she looked a lot like Lorena, the scattered, neurotic congresswoman who had rented our apartment.

Umberto didn't respond. He was tired and craving a hot shower. As we made our way into the building and waited for the elevator, Umberto danced around. He really had to pee.

"It's good to be back!" Umberto sighed expectantly when the building's tiny elevator finally groaned to a stop at our floor. He slipped the key in our front door, and the door creaked open. But before we could enter, something powerful knocked us back on our heels. It was like a punch to the gut. The strong odor of cat urine blasted into the hallway, along with impressive tufts of cat-hair which might be considered tumbleweeds if it had been the desert. The smell was so strong we had to hold our breath. Like firemen entering a burning building, we squared our shoulders and rushed in (but without masks) to open the windows.

We glanced around in dismay. Everything was dirty, dusty, and dingy. The floors were carpeted in animal fur. The furniture was coated with a thick layer of grime. The wall of the small bathroom had turned into one solid sheet of green mold, as Lorena had not kept the window cracked during Rome's humid winter. In the kitchen, the counter, already graying and chipped, was bruised by a nasty burn mark seared into its laminate border, a final, brutal insult. And this had happened in just two months. We should have known. What else could you expect of an Italian politician? Certainly, this explained a lot about the state of the Italian government.

After the initial clean-up and airing out of the apartment, I turned to Umberto. Lorena's stay in the apartment had changed the game for me. It was the final straw.

"Something's got to give," I said. "This place doesn't feel like home. It feels like a warehouse! I know we can't do any major renovation, but can't we at least make it cute somehow?"

This was my lifelong problem. I always wanted things to be cute. I could never suppress the desire to improve.

If a major renovation was not in the cards, at least we could get rid of years of accumulated grime and muck, I told myself. The apartment was never going to be the one of our dreams, but we could make it funky and warm and lived-in, couldn't we? There was a good chance that Umberto would end up teaching in Rome someday, in which case Rome would become our full-time home. And now, after the havoc that Lorena had wrought, it seemed the time to try to do something with the place.

With a renewed sense of dedication, we came up with a plan. The first order of business was the kitchen. The kitchen had never been renovated in all its 100 years. An unsightly hot water heater hulked high up in the center of one wall, in violation of recent building codes that dictated, rightly so, that these monstrosities be placed outside, just in case they should explode and disfigure someone. Six pipes splayed across the room.

Clearly, the kitchen needed help. The oven barely functioned. You made your *lasagna al forno* at the risk of death. The refrigerator's best days had long passed. The white paint (painted over the tile to cover hideous navy-blue tile which had been painted over the original abominable tile) had yellowed to the color of urine when you're very well hydrated. Of course, everything was dusty and disorderly too. We hadn't spent more than a week at one time in the apartment in several years, and Lorena's presence had not helped.

"Let's do a 50s look," I suggested to Umberto.

If necessity is the mother of invention, we were going to invent an irreverent, funky kitchen that would knowingly wink at its own atrociousness, celebrating what it could of itself and its dysfunctional layout, grotesque water heater and tangle of ugly pipes. We would call it *retro vintage*.

Being able to course-correct the trajectory of your life in a finger snap was probably why I'd been so fixated on renovating over all these years. It was a simple way to spark a sense of agency. On one level the changes were so basic as to be superficial, and on another, they almost always led to someplace far deeper—like one of the TV makeover shows where a new haircut results in a whole new life.

In planning how we might tweak our kitchen, we settled on the pipes as the coup de grace. Presently, they were painted an inoffensive white, an effort to disguise their unsightly forms to blend in with the wall. But what if we highlighted them by painting them a shiny silver? That would show the world (or at least ourselves) that we were embracing the ugliness, going with utilitarianism of the space. It would set off all the other industrial and retro elements. It would be utterly chic.

After getting permission from the owner, who conceded that the apartment has not been touched since the time his father bought it about 50 years earlier, we went shopping. We picked out a stainless steel, commercial-look stove to replace the broken one and bought "*Omar*," an aluminum shelving unit from Ikea that provided better storage space and played off the aluminum pipes. We bought an oversized aluminum pendant lamp also at Ikea and discovered the kitchen's crowning touch in a neighborhood store—a pastel yellow, retro, 50-style fridge

Umberto spent two marathon days on his knees, installing black and white peel-and-stick tiles bought from the local Leroy Merlin store, a French Home Depot-like chain. I thought back to the wood-paneled ceiling in Sardinia and kept my fingers crossed that Umberto would not run out of steam before this project was done. Then we hired Pasquale, a slight, wizened man always in baggy painter's whites with a cigarette perpetually dangling from the side of his mouth. He had been charged with lifting our cheerless kitchen out of its misery using the power of paint.

It took three days to repaint the kitchen. It had taken Umberto two days to lay the floor. We'd spent a couple of days shopping for the new stove and fridge. Also important in our refurbishment was a system of bins for recycling. Unlike too many American cities that paid scant attention to ecology, (the U.S. produces 30 percent of the planet's total waste, although it makes up only 4 percent of the world's population) Rome had recently instituted a new law requiring all households to collect their organic discards in a special can to be collected in a dedicated bin on the street. Our new recycling system allowed us to separate glass from plastic, paper and food waste and took up only a small corner of our small kitchen. In just a little bit more than a week, the kitchen was transformed. The new paint job, the checkerboard floors, the funky fridge, bestowed a sense of sauciness and attitude on what had been a very dreary space. Even the new stove slid between the countertops tidily, masking the burn mark the congresswoman left behind. Finally, the place felt like more of a home. And I, like the protagonist in one of those fashion makeover shows, felt more like my best self.

Lesson learned. I had always thought we needed a major renovation to live in the Rome apartment happily. As it turned out, transformation on a much smaller scale worked just fine, too.

HOME # FIVE
A BASEMENT APARTMENT
ON MELVIN AVENUE

Spending years living in two places, months at a time, in Sardinia, usually the warmer months, when the island was alive with activity and alternating with cold months in Boston—we eventually arrived at a point in our lives where we noticed our bank account was fattening up. And this was despite the countless renovation projects we had undertaken in both Sardinia and Boston.

Checking out our bank account online one afternoon, I told Umberto, "We need to invest the savings we've built up. It can't just sit around in a bank account doing nothing."

I was very practical about these sorts of things. I hated thinking about money, but I also had a thrifty streak that liked to maximize the little money we earned. Oh, I knew we were privileged, owning so many houses. We belonged to the tail end of a generation that had benefited from reasonable education and housing costs. I didn't have student loans, and rents and mortgages still consumed less than a third of our income. Life wouldn't be so easy for the next generation. But the fact that we were privileged only emphasized the duty we had not to squander our good luck.

"Yes," Umberto responded, "But where?" I don't want to buy stock."

Umberto was also thrifty and wanted to maximize what we had. But he was conservative when it came to investments, as was I. Both of us remained leery of the stock market after the crash of 2008. I had never understood complicated financial vehicles, and I trusted them even less after it became apparent what a scam so many of those investments actually were. The stock market was out.

The housing market, on the other hand, was something I could easily grasp. I understood bricks and mortar. I had watched various members of my own family thrive and prosper over the years in this world of cement, wood, and stucco. The trick, from what I could observe, was to buy something one could truly afford in a solid location in which there was high rental demand, preferably in a city with an economy diverse enough to protect it from any recessionary dips and slumps. Boston, with its prestigious universities, world-renowned hospitals, ever-growing biotechnology sector, and a burgeoning new start-up culture, would seem to be that place. With each passing year, the changes in the fabric of the city became more evident. Once a scrappy, insular, gritty town of residents who had never ventured beyond the safety of their own neighborhoods, it had become a dense, urban pudding of international students and immigrants from around the world. Certainly, it was wealthier than it once was. When I drove my almost 20-year-old Toyota out to Boston after college to accept my first job decades earlier, the city was pocked with vacant lots and rusted chain-link fences. Abandoned factories dominated many neighborhoods, a reminder of the city's manufacturing past. A methadone clinic in Kenmore Square attracted addicts who nervously prowled the streets alongside drunken college students on their way to the infamously seedy Rathskeller nightclub. Near Chinatown, the "Combat Zone" (the city's red-light district) was still in full swing as prostitutes sashayed down streets in hot pants and long, blonde wigs. Now glitzy new condominium buildings bearing "luxury living" banners rose in those very same neighborhoods, like gilded mushrooms in the city's newly-revitalized fertile humus.

Clearly, in this hopeful environment, our best move would be to buy whatever little hovel we could afford and rent it out. The rent would help insulate against the uncertainties of my freelance writing career. Hopefully, the property could at least maintain its value, which appeared to be no problem in Boston's heady biotech rush. Having an affinity for real estate, I brushed off the concerns of friends who told me again and again how they, themselves, would never want to be a landlord. We started shopping around.

We began making the rounds to open houses again. This time, we didn't bother with a realtor. For one thing, we were ashamed of how little we had to spend. Although we had built up money in the bank, it really wasn't *that* much money. Or at least, it wasn't by Boston standards. Boston was a high-cost city and had always been so. The city's burgeoning renaissance only made it pricier. The reality was that with the extra money we had saved that was banging around in the bank, we could only afford the tiniest little studio, a "property" that would not be considered worthy of the name in many other cities around the world. And unfortunately, there weren't a whole lot of these tiny apartments out there. Landlords, it seemed, found them too easy to manage, too easy to rent, too easy to bring in a nice fat profit if they had owned them long enough. Struggling just to find an apartment we could look at, we didn't need the added pressure of an agent, even one as relaxed as Matt, sending us an avalanche of real estate listings.

After a few months of looking, something unexpected happened. By an elaborate series of circumstances, it turned out that a basement studio in the building where we lived was to be sold. The condo association had decided to sell the unit to raise funds to convert the building from costly oil heat to less expensive gas heat. Through the strange machinations of tax law, it had turned out that the association would pay no taxes on the sale if the unit were sold to someone who already owned a unit in the building. The property manager sent out a notice to all unit owners offering the apartment for sale and announcing when bids were due.

Umberto and I quickly set up an appointment to visit the apartment.

Seeing the "apartment" was a bit of a surreal experience. It was the size of a single bedroom, only about 350 square feet, and very dingy. It reeked of stale cigarette smoke, dirty laundry, and the tenant's open whiskey bottles. The tenant had furnished the unit sparsely and inattentively, with one large, unmade bed, a broken bureau, a battered coffee table, and one huge 50-inch television which dominated the center of the room. Large radiator and building pipes extended across the length of one wall. In the kitchen, a cheap laminate counter accented greasy 1970s era beige cabinets and very old appliances, also encrusted with layers of cooking oil. The cabinets were not in terrible shape, but they too were covered in several decades worth of Crisco. Beneath the sink, an old paint bucket caught the incessant drip of water leaking from a busted pipe. The tenant had used pieces of silver duct tape to "repair" cracks in the wall. An obscenely dirty wall-to-wall carpet was the apartment's one nod to comfort. Along the borders where the carpet met the wall was a trail of mouse excrement.

To be honest, in that moment, it was hard to see the potential in the place. This was the type of apartment that would give me the legitimate new title of "slumlord." I would be ashamed to own the place. But maybe, just perhaps, we could work with all of this?

"I don't know," Umberto said as we emerged from the filthy basement. He breathed in and sighed loudly. "Is that really worth investing in?"

I didn't know either, but I did know that there was nothing cheaper on the market in the city of Boston. And this was all we could afford.

"Yes," I told him. For maybe the first time in all the time we had known each other, *I* was the optimistic one. "Although the apartment is a basement it's actually "garden level," I said. "It's got four full windows that get a decent amount of light. It's even direct light! And yeah, the apartment is the size of a toenail, but the kitchen is a reasonable size. It's the same kitchen you might find in any one-bedroom apartment."

Was I trying to convince Umberto, or trying to convince myself?

The kitchen even included a breakfast bar for two, eliminating the need for a dining table. There were two built-in closets and though the bathroom would need to be redone (as the tenant had decided to cement the toilet base to the linoleum floor in a strange attempt to fix a leak) at least there *was* a bathroom.

Jittery, wondering if we were about to make one of the biggest mistakes of our lives, we decided to bid on the dump. In previous months, we had made offers on several different small studios around town and lost out each time to eager buyers willing to pay tens of thousands above the asking price, just for the privilege of owning a little piece of Boston. Because this unit was not listed in the MLS, the number of bidders would be limited, reducing the likelihood of a repeat of that type of scenario.

In the end, only one other party, another woman who owned a unit in the building, was interested in making an offer. All the other potential buyers had probably been scared off by the apartment's pitiful condition. Or perhaps they simply felt that owning one unit in our ramshackle building was enough.

The property manager informed us that bids were due by 5 p.m. on a Wednesday afternoon in June. We were to make our best and final offers in writing. The association was insisting that all offers be proffered with no contingencies and no inspection. Let the buyer beware. Having been burned several times before by submitting bids below asking, this time, we decided to go for broke. We would bid above asking for this cesspool of a place. But by how much? Looking around at studios in the previous months, we knew that the asking price was within range but no bargain for a basement unit in that kind of condition. Offering too much above asking-price seemed risky. On the other hand, we were reasonably certain that we would not be able to find a comparable unit for a comparable price on the open market. A few weeks before this unit had become available, another basement unit in the same complex only slightly larger, had sold for about $50,000 more.

The month that bids came due, we were in Sardinia, but my calendar was marked. I called a friend back in Boston, who had a good head for business.

"How much are taxes and the condo fee?" he queried.

I told him.

"How much would you charge for rent?"

I told him what I thought we could get based on sifting through Craigslist ads in the neighborhood.

"In that case," he said, "I think you could offer as much as $10,000 more than asking and you would still be getting a very decent 6 percent return. "

Now we were talking.

Still, $10,000 more than asking was far above what I had imagined offering for the place. To my mind, the asking price was already stretching the limits. Knowing the Boston housing market, I had accepted that our offer would need to go higher, but I was thinking of something on the order of $5,000 more, not $10,000. After nervously mulling it over, we took the advice of my friend and plunged into the deep end of the pool. We bid $10,125 over asking. (The $125 was just to bump us up over the $10,000 threshold in case our competitor had the same idea.)

That night, as we had in the past, we brooded over our latest real estate adventure.

"Are you sure we aren't making a mistake?" I asked Umberto. I was less optimistic now.

"They probably won't take it," he reassured me.

The next day, an email message blinked into my inbox. It was from M & P Property Management Association. I held my breath and clicked on it.

"Congratulations Pam! You submitted the highest bid," it read.

It turned out my friend had been right. Our competitor had bid $8,000 over asking, and we would have lost out if we had stuck with our original, more conservative plan. I would have him to thank—or berate—depending on how this whole thing turned out.

We took one year to ponder changes as the tenant finished out his lease. It was psychologically impossible for us to leave the current tenant in place and the apartment in its current degraded state, as most landlords would. We were fixers. We were doers. Our philosophy had always been to leave the world in a better condition than we'd found it, even a 350-square foot rattrap. I did not want to be a slumlord, nor even a typical landlord, renovating with the cheapest materials, assuming a tenant would destroy anything better. Instead, I wanted to try having a little faith in the world of the faithless, imagining that any tenant living in an apartment that had been shone love and respect would treat the apartment with love and respect in kind. Call it property karma. Perhaps that was why the last tenant, caught in a circle of neglect and carelessness, had been so unkind to the apartment. It was bad karma.

Beyond the philosophical motives of a renovation, we had a business interest as well. We wanted to expand the potential rental pool. With the ratty carpeting, dilapidated kitchen and cheap finishes, the best tenant we could ever hope to attract would be an ascetic, perhaps a student, poor and neglectful or simply immune to creature comforts, cloistered in a dungeon while trying to make the semester's tuition. I wanted the possibility of renting to adults who might be less transient, and who might transform the place into a real home. For me to be a happy landlord, I needed to rent out a place where I, myself, would be happy to live.

I had pictures of the place that we took the very first time we visited. Since we couldn't visit the apartment very often, the pictures helped us envision the changes we needed to make.

"First off, we've got to change that carpeting," said Umberto, studying the photograph we had taken. There was so much dirty laundry on the floor in the picture, you could hardly see the carpeting. But I remembered it without the photo. It was *brutto*. Stained and industrial, it was the type of cheap, gray carpet you see in car rental offices. I also remembered it was saturated with the odor of cigarette smoke and peppered with mouse turds. It was completely unsanitary.

"Why don't we use the kind of porcelain tile we used on the kitchen in Sardinia?" I asked. "Let's do it in a herringbone pattern!"

I was getting excited. I was warming up to the new blank canvas we had to work with.

"It makes sense to replace it with a hard surface," agreed Umberto. "It's easier to clean, will withstand good and bad tenants and it can stand up to possible leaks."

Leaks, of course, were an inescapable risk in basement apartments.

Renovations began the following May. By this time, we had formulated a plan of attack.

The wall of pipes, we decided, made the apartment feel more basement-like than ever while consuming valuable wall space that could have otherwise been used for storage. And besides, these were not the "cool" pipes of design magazines that could be painted silver or red like something in a Restoration Hardware catalog. That's something we had tried, successfully, in Rome. But these pipes were of plastic and enfolded in insulation wrapping.

Umberto spent more nights hunched before the computer, designing a detailed drawing of a built-in wall unit that could hide all the ugly pipes and the radiator attached to the wall, while providing storage that was essential in a studio apartment.

And of course, the kitchen needed a major overhaul. We could leave the current configuration in place, but we would have to rip out the vinyl flooring, the grease-encrusted appliances, the tired old cabinets and laminate countertop. No self-respecting tenant would want to touch anything in that kitchen.

The day that *1-800-Got Junk?* came to haul away all the old contents of the apartment, broken toilet and all, felt like some sort of special holiday. We had been waiting for this. And was it my imagination, or did the apartment seem to hold an anticipative air? You could feel it. For the apartment, too, there was renewed hope. Spring sunshine rushed in through the newly-uncovered windows to underscore the fact.

Scott, a carpenter we had hired on the recommendation of a friend from the dog park, got busy with preparing a subfloor that would be rigid enough to accept a new floor. We opted for resistant, hard-wearing tile, a Marazzi white-washed, wood-look tile with the name "Montagna" that we hoped would help the space feel lighter, larger, and a tad more refined. Real wood might have been our first choice in a street-level apartment, but in a basement unit we felt both wood and laminate could be easily damaged if water should wash in after a heavy rain, as it had been known to do in other basement units in the neighborhood. In the end, though, we skipped the herringbone design. Scott informed us that the extra work in that little flourish would substantially raise the cost of installation.

With his blond ponytail swinging down his back, Scott spent several days on his knees, laying tile, then grouting. With this one simple change, the apartment, like the scarecrow in the Wizard of Oz, was magically transformed. Before, it had been only a forlorn bedroom, one inspection away from legal action. Now, it felt larger, almost stately. It had self-respect. Did houses and apartments have feelings? My mystical side said yes. Somehow, bare walls responded to the energy of the people contained within them. Like everyone and everything else, they responded to love and attention, too.

Within three weeks, most of the work had been completed. Scott built a custom cabinet to box in the pipes and provide storage shelves. We added a simple white Ikea wardrobe, a TV cabinet, a dresser and desk that gave the wall a clean, well-planned functionality. The popcorn finish ceiling was removed, the walls were painted a fresh cream. New kitchen cabinets were installed, a new Corian countertop and breakfast bar, along with a new shower box, a new vanity, and toilet in the bathroom, and new appliances in the kitchen. A glass tile backsplash, beige and brown, with flecks of blue, added just the right accent. The apartment, although modest and diminutive in size, now had what it had been missing all these years—dignity. Even before the last nail was driven, the apartment was quickly rented by a courteous young professional who eagerly moved in one summer evening with the help of his friends, and thereafter treated the place like home. I was happy, the tenant was happy, and the apartment was happy, you could just feel it.

HOME # SIX
AN APARTMENT
ON PENNSYLVANIA AVENUE
(NOT THE WHITE HOUSE)

One day in August, Umberto and I were sitting on a beautiful beach in Sardinia, a few months before we were to receive a phone call that would completely change the structure of our lives. And it was a good thing, too, because the structure of our lives, in recent years, had become as rickety as one of our patio chairs.

We had reached an impasse.

We were at Porto Conte, a small, almost hidden inlet with a wonderful feel of seclusion that stood in contrast to the fashionably trendy and therefore packed sandy stretches closer to Alghero. The sun was setting, and I couldn't help but beat back the impression that the sun was setting on our relationship as well. We were in the midst of another uncomfortable discussion of the type we'd been having more and more of lately. Part of it had to do with our lives, complicated by living in two places at once. Part of it had to do with who we were becoming.

As usual, the house was at the center of everything.

"I think a problem I have is the complexity of it," I said to Umberto, digging my toes into the sand. "Maybe if we could find a nice, simple apartment in downtown Alghero I would feel more comfortable."

Umberto lay face down, motionless on his beach towel.

Even after all these years, the Alghero house still felt unknowable, a mystery that would forever escape my technological grasp. I still hadn't learned all the complex, labyrinthine systems, and I knew that if I were ever to stay there for any extended period alone, I would not be able to do it. If Umberto wasn't around, I would need to rely on the services of Claudio. I found this unsettling as the odds increase with each passing year that one of us would indeed be living in the house alone one day. Alone, one of us would have to perilously balance on the chair above the basement stairs to reset the cistern. Alone, one of us would have to climb the narrow spiral steps to the second floor. If either of us slipped and fell (as has happened once when I was younger and more elastic) we'd be on our own for days, until hopefully Claudio would come by to discover a heap of the bones long-ago picked clean by wild boars.

"But there's nothing out there!" Umberto said, sitting up. "We've looked! And I don't want to give up our place to go live in one of those ugly and anonymous buildings in Alghero!"

We'd been over this well-worn topic time and time again.

And he was right about what he said. We had looked over the years, during periods in which I had felt particularly burdened by house and garden worries. What we found was even more depressing than what we had seen during our first house-hunting foray more than 20 years ago. Bad layouts. Dated finishes. Noisy locations. And worst of all, high prices that could in no way, by any stretch of the imagination, be justified. With the kind of housing prices we were seeing, we couldn't afford to move, even if we could manage to sell our place for five times what we had paid for it.

"Besides," he added, "you wouldn't be happy even in an apartment in Alghero. You would still say that Sardinia is too small and too homogeneous."

That kind of talk always infuriated me. How could *he* presume to know how I would feel when even *I* didn't know how I would feel? What *was* true, though, was that over the years, going back and forth between two continents, I had seen my life in the U.S. flourish, while my life in Sardinia seemed to be atrophying. It wasn't hard to understand why. First, after three years of casting about for a regular income anywhere in the world, I had finally gotten a job, part-time, in Boston. I knew that it was to be only temporary, but after such a long period of being unemployed, I was simply grateful and relieved to have a job, even if it meant no more travel to Sardinia for a while. Sometime after I took the job, a health problem surfaced, and I much preferred to tend to it at one of Boston's preeminent teaching hospitals, not the ill-equipped, prison-atmosphere hospital available to me in Sardinia.

Meanwhile, Umberto's job, responsibilities and social status in Sardinia had grown. He couldn't take much time away. As a result of all this, I was spending more time in Boston, and Umberto was spending more time in Sardinia. Our time together seemed to be getting shorter and shorter each year. This was putting a severe strain on our relationship. The ground seemed to be shifting under our feet, along with our goals, desires, and direction in life. It no longer seemed so compelling, at least to me, to put all of my attention on nesting in the Sardinian countryside.

A lot had changed since that first ferry ride to Sardinia, more than 20 years earlier. The house was different, the island was different, and we were different. Our first dog Tony had given way to Oliver, and even Oliver was getting older. With time and age, I felt I had a better handle on what I could expect to change in life, what would remain the same, and where I should concentrate my energies and expectations. As much as I stewed over it, Sardinia did not seem to be that place.

While Umberto felt this on some level, the reality of life was that his job was still in Sardinia. Over the years, he had investigated other universities in other places, but the Italian university system was slow, and transferring to another university in another city on the mainland of Italy was neither a fast nor a simple thing. Entire glaciers were disappearing in the meantime. It didn't seem to make sense to live in Rome if Umberto's job was in Sardinia. And Boston was not realistic, not only because it was far too competitive to find a job at one of its universities but because it would mean that Umberto would have to sacrifice his standing in the Italian university system, which he didn't want to do, and I didn't blame him. Tenure and funding are both hard to come by in the American university system.

At the moment, I was willing to give the town experience of Sardinia a chance. Yes, a village in the interior had felt claustrophobic so many years ago. But I was willing to bet that living in a larger town on the coast, so many years later, would feel less so. Sardinia had changed a lot. RyanAir was now using Alghero as a hub, and during the tourist season, there were regular direct flights from Paris, Frankfurt, Stockholm, and Barcelona. Charter flights from Russia brought a flock of Russian tourists. The town now felt open to the world. If I lived in town, I told myself, not only could I mix and mingle with the newcomers, but I could take pleasant afternoon walks along the esplanade, without having to drive anywhere.

I'd have easy access to beachside bars and Old Town restaurants. I could visit the bustling outdoor market every day. And I'd always be attuned to whatever show or movie was coming to the theatre next because I would pass the flyers and posters on the street. I could at least try to fit into the fabric of Sardinian life in a way that was much more difficult living isolated out on our country "estate." Umberto, meanwhile, could happily keep stoking the roaring flames of his career. But, honestly, would this really be enough to make me happy? I was not sure of it, and even if things were a bit better in town, the reality was that I couldn't picture myself living full-time in Sardinia for the rest of my days. It would be hard to deny myself the excitement and sense of possibility that life in Boston offered. And then there was my family. My parents were in Las Vegas, and I had three nieces, now with their own kids and families, in Los Angeles. As I got older, it seemed like it would make sense to live closer to them, if not in the same town, at least the same country.

"You only want to live in Boston," said Umberto angrily. "Face it, you just don't want to live in Italy!"

Would this argument ever be over?

Again, I felt this wasn't true. I would renounce something very precious if I gave up on life in Italy. I loved how the Italians seemed to savor life in ways that Americans didn't. They were more relaxed, they were more congenial and lighthearted. Real-life, the life of emotions and connections between humans and nature, did not get obscured and lost, the way it seemed to in technology-obsessed, corporatized America. In America, people spent their most vital days worrying over their 401Ks. People's only brush with feelings came in overly sentimental TV commercials peddling prescription pills or life insurance. The emotional life in Italy was far more substantial, and people spent their time thinking about their next delicious meal, not retirement. In addition, there was a much deeper sense of being a steward of the planet. America had become wasteful, inefficient, profligate in its great wealth, with little concern about long-term costs to the environment or the world community. Italians, with a longer history and World War II fought on their soil, still maintained a sense of themselves in relationship to animals, nature, the environment, the world. There was a sense of humility. Though they enjoyed a comfortable life, they were not wasteful. In Italy, grocery store refrigerator and freezer bins had doors because it only made sense, while at the local Trader Joe's in the States, freezers, and refrigerators stood open, in a wasteful duel with the store's heating system. In Rome, "humid" waste—potato peelings, banana skins, and other assorted leftovers—were collected for composting, whereas in the States, many municipalities asked residents to carefully sort through their recyclables only to throw them all into the same groaning landfill. In the last analysis, in almost all respects, Italians seemed happier, more grounded, more conscientious. I would always want a piece of that in my life. At the same time, I would never feel the ease that I felt in the U.S. when negotiating new situations, people and places. In Italy, simple things could sometimes end up feeling more complicated.

In the U.S., I knew how to act, what to say, what to expect, even around people I had never met before. In

Italy, every transaction provoked anxiety. I thought back to the nightmare of getting a driver's license in Sardinia. I had driven for more than 20 years, including twice driving from one end of the U.S. to the other on my own, and yet at the time that I took a test for my driver's license, my Italian driving instructor managed to make me feel as if I were a swerving, skidding neophyte. He barked and growled at every intersection, clicked his tongue, and yelled. By the end of the test, my knees were shaking. It was hard to see this kind of thing happening in the U.S., where driving instructors seemed to have better things to do with their time than intimidate and bully students. Besides, on average, people seemed to be better drivers in the U.S. anyway without all the theatrics.

These kinds of things I could live without, although they did lend Italy a certain capricious charm in comparison to the bland uniformity of the U.S. I really wanted a taste of *both* places, and I couldn't quite see giving up the U.S. forever.

And so, we were at a stalemate.

"I don't know how to fix this," I said to Umberto. "If we find a house in town, I think I would feel better there, and I would be willing to live there *part* of the year. I just can't say I would be willing to live there full-time."

"But my job is *here!*" Umberto reiterated. "I've looked for jobs in the U.S. and nothing has come through. And besides, jobs in the U.S. can end at any time."

"Maybe this is it," I told Umberto sadly. "Maybe we've reached the end of the road. Maybe we were meant to be together for the period of time we were together, and now it's over."

I had long ago developed a philosophy of marriage as a partnership in which partners were to encourage each other's personal growth and development. And right now, right here, I couldn't help but think that we were actually standing in each other's way. But I had been through enough in life, enough of having to let go of things I preferred to keep, to recognize that I couldn't cling to something if it was not meant to be. Clinging was in direct contradiction to what the Chinese refer to as the "Tao," and so many years ago, I had named my first dog Tao for a reason. One of the undeniable truths of the universe was that you must let go of dearly loved things, people, situations. There is no way around this. So you could either choose to let go gracefully, adapting and moving fluidly from one position to another, like a peaceful yogi in a hot room. Or, alternatively, you could clutch fiercely to people, places, situations, that once were, but that were fading fast. And let's be honest, clinging at all costs to the past, as with dyed hair that shows its gray roots, is frankly unbecoming.

We sat together on the beach, miserable in our silence.

We left our impasse unresolved that day. There was no clear direction to where we were headed and the path ahead seemed so obstructed by bramble it was impossible to see the way forward. A few months later, we visited my parents in Las Vegas. There it became clear to both Umberto and me that my parents' time to let go had also arrived. My mother had been sick for a while, with multiple myeloma, a form of cancer that was treatable but not curable. My father had been taking care of her. Upon retiring, while still only in their 50s, my parents had built an expansive 6-bedroom home with a resplendent swimming pool, a free-standing workshop/toolshed and a large independent "casita" that my father used as a photography studio. But now, after 20 plus years, their proud home, with all its many annexes, its front and back lawns, its swimming pool and its luxuriant mint-green carpeting, had become a mint-green prison. My mother couldn't manage the stairs, so she didn't leave the bedroom. My father, in the non-stop care required for my mother, was forgetting to pay bills and had let basic house maintenance lapse. He no longer had the energy to drag the big net out of the toolshed to pull leaves and drowned insects from their abandoned green pool. He no longer had the energy to cook, much less purge their loud and grimy refrigerator densely packed with multiple half-empty jars of taco sauce. Convincing my parents to downsize took some doing, but it was clear, even to them, that something had to give. The sheer and undeniable weight of the house had cracked my parent's hardened resolve to stay put. They agreed to downsize.

In what was perhaps one of the biggest tasks I had tackled in my lifetime, we moved to my parents' house for two months. We sifted through 60 years' worth of my parents' accumulations, which was a temporary diversion from the gargantuan, yawning chasm in our relationship. For a few weeks, Umberto and I set aside our grand dilemma and merged our energies to solve a different kind of problem with a very concrete, identifiable solution. But what kind of concrete solution was to be found for our own more fundamental existential predicament?

The day that we returned to Boston from Las Vegas, we arrived, as usual, bleary-eyed and ragged after an overnight red-eye flight. We could never sleep in the cramped plane, so we always felt jet-lagged and hungover after each trip. Our habit, if possible, was to catch a couple hours of sleep before starting the day in earnest.

And that's what we did this time. We both took showers and changed into our pajamas for a mid-morning nap. About halfway through it, we were awakened by the shrill ring of Umberto's cell phone. Why hadn't he turned that darned thing off?

It was a call from Italy. Umberto responded to it, although I would have encouraged him to let it go to voicemail. I could tell by Umberto's voice it was someone important.

"*Si. Si. Certo,*" said Umberto on his end. He was using his professional tone that was meant to suggest competence and efficiency.

It turned out it was the Italian Ministry of Foreign Affairs. They had a question for Professor De Angelis. The *Professore* had applied for a position as science attaché at the Italian Embassy in Washington a couple of years back. And true, the *Professore* had not been selected for the position at that time, despite the fact that it was the second time he had applied for it and was eminently qualified. But there had been a bit of a change in circumstances, a *piccolo imprevisto*. It seems the candidate who had accepted the position had, at the last minute, had to withdraw, due to an illness in the family. Therefore, the position was now open. No one at the Ministry felt it made sense to re-open a search for a whole new group of candidates, as this would delay filling the position for several more years. The decision had been made to return to the list of finalist candidates during the last call. The *Professore* had come in second in the selection process.

So the question was this: Would Professor De Angelis be interested in serving as the Italian science attaché in Washington DC? Take a day or two. Think about it.

Umberto clicked off the phone in an incredulous daze, and we looked at each other, dumbfounded. It was clearly a gift from the Universe, resolving most of our issues in one fortuitous ring of the cell phone, at least for a while. The elegance of this solution, its unexpectedness and perfect timing, was almost eerie given that had the Ministry personnel tried to call even just one day earlier during our time in Las Vegas, they would not have reached us. If they had tried, they would have called at 3 a.m., and Umberto's phone would have been switched off. If they had called even a few days earlier, we would have been preoccupied with getting my parents' home repainted and re-carpeted before putting it up for sale and flying out of town. It might have been days before Umberto would have seen the call. We had been overloaded with my parents' changes in the last few months, there had been no mental space for anything else, but now, finally, there was time to think about our own.

Certainly, this was some sort of a sign? Or maybe just a karmic reward for all our work in Vegas?

"So," Umberto turned to me, "how do you feel about moving to Washington?"

I didn't know how to respond. I didn't know much about Washington, other than a friend of mine who lived there was quick to correct me whenever I lapsed by calling it DC.

"Here, we call it The District," she reprimanded.

So now I knew what to call it. That was all I knew. It was not much more than I knew about Sardinia when we first took the leap to move there nearly 20 years ago. But if there were ever a time to take another big risk, this seemed to be it.

Still, we were afraid of many things, more so this time around than the first time. Umberto was spooked by the confinement of a traditional "desk" job requiring 9 to 5 hours and the straitjacket of a suit and tie. Plus, he would now be a diplomat and would be required to give up his hard-won green card. Who would watch the house in Sardinia? What would we do with the condo in Boston?

And how would we play landlord from long distance? I was nervous about leaving a familiar structure in Boston, one I had worked long and hard to maintain in the face of our moves back and forth between Boston and Sardinia all these years. Now, we would both be living full-time, together in one place, for better or worse. Would we even get along? We had only experienced twelve-months a year, full-time life together in those earliest years in Sardinia. There would be no release valve anymore. We would both be leaving our comfort zones, although I would have the advantage of living in my native country while Umberto would have the advantage of working in Italian, among his own people. Plus, the cafeteria at the Italian Embassy served an incredibly authentic Italian pizza. But a move like this seemed in keeping with the theme of my life if my life had had one. It had been about being courageous enough (or maybe foolish enough) to leave a well-paid job that just didn't feel right anymore. It had been about leaping into change, inviting it, initiating it, but understanding as well that not everything could be changed or should be. It was about balancing change and stasis by taking the time to fully live experiences as they happened, not thinking too far into the future. Sometimes, it was about thinking about the future. It was about offering up yourself to the world, as I did as a painter displaying my art on a wall, with the faith that someone out in the world would understand what I was offering and find it worthwhile. Sometimes, the inner voice urging you forward was barely audible. Sometimes its screams were ear-splitting. But the important thing was to listen to it.

If before in my life, space and place had served as a reflection of my identity, if the building and shaping of houses and apartments had been a physical manifestation of the building of my relationship with Umberto and a physical sign of my own evolution, if I had learned in the doing what could be considered "real" and what would remain only fantasy, well, now I was approaching a different phase. It was a phase of acceptance, in which questions of style and identity had somehow been integrated into my core and were therefore more intuitive and required less reflection. By now, Umberto and I knew who we are, and by now, we knew what we could expect from each other and what would forever remain a fantasy. There was a sort of freedom in all that too. We no longer pined away for things that would never be.

And so, in this spirit, Umberto accepted the Ministry's invitation. We got back on Craigslist, scouring ads for the perfect DC rental. It was not so easy to find what we knew by now was "our" kind of space—not cookie-cutter or run-of-the-mill, but a place in the heart of the city that was interesting enough, airy, and just big enough (but no bigger) to contain our non-cookie-cutter lives.

It was incredible to think we were doing this all over again, and yet here we were.

After relatively little searching, we found a place. In another stroke of what felt like fate, it happened to be an apartment we saw a couple of weeks after that first unlikely phone call from the ministry. Both of us, instantaneously, knew we fit there. The apartment was a corner unit with nearly wall-to-wall windows, high ceilings, and shiny wooden floors. It had a fireplace, a balcony, and fortunately, for elderly Oliver, an elevator. Renovating this time was out of the question. But somehow, after all these years and countless home improvement projects, I was okay with that. Some part of me would probably always seek to make things better somewhere, but I had reached a stage in life where that somewhere might be the world, rather than my home.

That's not to say we've given up on house and home. I've heard that the French furniture outlet Maison du Monde is having a big sale. And we've got an empty apartment waiting for us. We're 50 and should know better, but we're still excited.

This time around, we're going for the industrial look.

REVAMP

EPILOGUE

The artistic journey that began with a deformed drawing of a skeleton at the Accademia di Belle Arti in Sassari, Italy in 1998 continues as of the writing of this book (2019). I'm still painting. I've moved through a number of wildly divergent styles, enjoying every twist and turn along the way. Gallery owners, I am sure, roll their eyes. They prefer one recognizable, brandable "look." It's easier to sell a name that way. But what's the point for the artist? Where's the exploration? Where's the risk and discovery?

Space is an ongoing problem. I have yet to find a solution to the always growing number of canvases in my studio that breed and regenerate like love-crazed rabbits. Sadly, sales are not keeping up with production. In fact, I am making the problem worse. I have gotten into sculpture, and I now have a number of clay figures balefully glaring at me for their rightful place—on a shelf on the floor? on the table?—in our home and Umberto patiently accepts it. Sometimes, I think I ought to just quit making art altogether. Am I adding more "stuff" to the world that will just end up in a landfill?

I've finally found a way to marry my twin passions of art and writing. For years I struggled to find work that I could do from most anywhere I happened to be. After teaching English and a few translation jobs, I ended up working for a while doing editorial work at a lab in Boston, and after that, working as an associate editor of a science and technology magazine. I loved that the magazine allowed me to work from both the United States and Europe, but frankly, I was not in love with the subject matter. Neural imaging, big data, robotics, and artificial intelligence are not my thing. Today, I write on the visual arts, and it finally feels like the right fit. When I began painting, I was loathe to take on the role of analyzing something that I wanted to be a purely intuitive undertaking. I did not want to pick apart other people's art-making, especially since it can be such a personal thing, to begin with. Who has the right, really, to criticize someone else's personal journey?

Now, while I still feel uncomfortable playing art critic (and I generally avoid what would strictly be considered art criticism), I do enjoy my self-defined mission of introducing the public to artists who seldom get much attention. I avoid "art speak" at all costs in favor of talking to artists about their art using plain language. Art often cannot be described in words, but certainly impenetrable, pompous explanations don't help matters any. Overblown language is a way of hiding from art, not embracing it. Furthermore, it does nothing to help viewers to really "see."

I don't read shelter magazines very much anymore, but I still buy a lot of art books. Sometimes, I ponder how I'm doing the two things I love most—making art and writing about it—thanks only to my time in Sardinia. What's ironic is that Sardinia, while providing the initial spark for what I do now, is not the place that allows for its fullest expression.

Of course, Sardinia itself has changed a great deal from my earliest days there, and parts of Sardinia that I describe in the book (roughly between 1995 through about 2010) might be unrecognizable today. Things are more modern, a little bit more like everywhere else in the world. Italy is in many ways very different from the country it once was, grappling with questions around immigration, ethnicity and race that were much less acknowledged when I first arrived.

The names of most of the characters in the book, including that of my husband, have been changed. Most of our friends, thankfully, are still alive and working continuously on improving their spaces.

My life of traveling, moving, renovating, and making art, has taught me so many lessons that stay with me, no matter where I happen to live. One of the most powerful of these is this: It's up to each of us to make a work of art while we can, not just of our immediate surroundings, but of our lives. Home is where the "art" is.

ACKNOWLEDGMENTS

More than I could ever have realized when I first set out to write a book about a life viewed through the lens of home renovation, I now understand that writing a book, like building a house, is a collaborative experience.

As much as I have relied on roofers, carpenters, and tilers, over the years, I have relied on friends and supporters to help shape a vague idea into a finished manuscript.

Thanks to my husband, "Umberto" for being my accomplice in crime all these years. Without you, of course, there would have been no book, and I would never have known the stark beauty of Sardinia. Thanks for greeting every project and idea enthusiastically over the years, including this book. You were the first reader and undoubtedly, the only person featured in nearly every scene.

Thanks to Linda Sanders, my dog-walking companion, who has great taste in literature and who graciously volunteered to read an early draft of this book before I could even ask. It was her recommendation to read Elena Ferrante that ultimately inspired me to begin writing this book one winter's morning in Rome.

Thanks to Karen Gross, who told me she would be "honored" to read the book, although she has a busy career writing books of her own. Like an experienced electrician, her insightful rewiring helped provide some snap, crackle, and pop.

Thanks to Ed Siegel for his penetrating intellect, quiet wisdom and support at various stages of writing. Thanks also to Curt Eriksen, who spent countless hours listening to my gripes and frustrations about the world of publishing, and to Jane Simon who provided expert graphic design advice. Thanks also to Susan Pollack, who, although she didn't edit this book, read it, and provided savvy advice and lots of encouragement.

And thanks, finally, to all the friends in my life, (including the furry ones), both in Italy and the United States, too many to name here, who have been with me in love and laughter, before the walls came down and after. You have made my life richer in every respect... and I've stolen some good design ideas from you too.

NOTE FROM THE AUTHOR

Word-of-mouth is crucial for any author to succeed. If you enjoyed the book, please leave a review online—anywhere you are able. Even if it's just a sentence or two. It would make all the difference and would be very much appreciated.

Thanks!
Pamela

ABOUT THE AUTHOR

Pamela Reynolds is an award-winning writer and artist who has written for numerous lifestyle magazines and blogs. Formerly a writer and editor at The Boston Globe, she currently writes on the visual arts for WBUR, an NPR affiliate in Boston. Pamela studied painting in Italy. Her paintings belong to several corporate collections and were featured in two major motion pictures. She has added Washington D.C. to her list of "hometowns."

Find out more at www.pamreynolds.com.

Thank you so much for reading one of our *TRAVEL MEMOIR* novels. If you enjoyed our book, please check out our recommended title for your next great read!

Cucina Tipica by Andrew Cotto

"Whether you love Italy, dream of visiting it one day (like myself) or just want to enjoy an incredibly enjoyable book set in a beautiful part of the world, I thoroughly recommend this story as the best I have ever read!"
– *Midwest Book Review*

View other Black Rose Writing titles at
www.blackrosewriting.com/books and use promo code
PRINT to receive a **20% discount** when purchasing.

www.ingramcontent.com/pod-product-compliance
Lightning Source LLC
Chambersburg PA
CBHW052028070526
44584CB00016B/1956